Groceryman

Robert Lee Hamady

ISBN 0-9785579-0-5
Printed in the United States of America

For Lewie, Sarah, Leslie, Alex and Sophie

PREFACE

In Flint, Michigan, there was a family grocery business called Hamady Bros. Founded in 1911 by Michael Hamady with his cousin Kamol, Druze immigrants from Lebanon, the company grew to have $100,000,000 in annual revenue, employing 1300 employees. *In Flint for Flint* was its motto, and working in the stores became a rite of passage. Said one employee in a Flint Journal article, "'The question was did we go to work at G.M. or Hamady's.... We'd think, well, at G.M. there's strikes and layoffs. But everybody's got to eat.'" And most everyone got their eats at Hamadys.

"Shirtsleeves to shirtsleeves," Michael Hamady told everyone, by which he meant that he would be followed into the business by his son, then by his son's sons and their descendants in a never ending line. Generations of Hamadys would come and go but Hamady Bros. would endure.

It didn't turn out that way. But for me, it might have. And so, I wrote this book.

R.L.H.

I

In 1966 when I was thirty and still in college, my mother called. "Your father is ill," she said. "I'll tell you more when I see you. Come home." She hung up. I called back but she didn't pick up.

Ann Arbor to Flint is a one hour drive north. The fields were yellow now and the corn was down. Another week and Dad might call to hunt pheasants on Valender's farm. The family business bought Valender's celery, so my father could hunt it and any number of farms between Flint and Saginaw or Port Huron. Strange that Mother hadn't inflated Dad's illness and blamed me for it as she'd done when he had his bleeding ulcers. Now she was mysterious. What did *that* portend? He was only 58. And in the one-man family business that had 1300 employees, he was the man. If Dad was sick, Hamady Bros. was sick.

Mother was not at home. "Go to McLaren Hospital," her maid told me. "And you must see Dr. Chambers *before* seeing your father."

McLaren is a quiet suburban hospital on Flint's West side. When the doctor came down to answer his page, we shook hands in silence and I followed him into an empty office. He sat behind a desk and gazed at me with folded hands before he spoke.

"Your father came to see me three days ago," he began quietly, confidentially. "He had on dark glasses. He said the light hurt his eyes. He wanted a prescription for headaches. The strongest you've got, he said. I asked him where he'd come from. He didn't remember. He couldn't say where he'd parked his car. He didn't know what day it was. How he was able to drive there I don't know. I called for an ambulance and had him admitted. He's been seen by two neurologists. He's had x-rays. I have the radiologist's report. I think we're all agreed...."

He paused to judge how frank he could be.

"... There's a large mass pressing against his brainstem. It doesn't look like an abscess. It looks to be aggressive, and it's inoperable. If the diagnosis is correct, there is no cure."

I took in a deep breath and let it slowly out. So, the old man's gonna die, I told myself. Better start getting used to it.

"How long has he got?" I asked.

"Days. Maybe a week.... I haven't told him. He's asking when he can get back to the business."

At the mention of the business the man we'd been talking about resolved clearly into my father. Tears welled under my eyes and the doctor nodded sympathetically. Yes, that man who was days away from brain death and wanted to get back to the business—that was my dad. To the core, a groceryman. I never knew him as anything else. Coming into my nursery long after I went to sleep I probably smelled him before I saw him, smelled that perfume from the produce house on his Arrow shirt: pascal celery, rutabagas, Michigan potatoes and sweat.

I went upstairs and walked down the corridor of mostly open rooms trying not to look in. The door to Dad's room was closed and I opened it slightly. Mother saw me and came out.

"Did you talk to Dr. Chambers?"

I nodded.

She laid her head on my shoulder and cried. "Honest to God, I had no idea. I thought it was stress. He hid it from everyone."

"Who's here?" Dad asked in a strange, slow monotone.

I entered. The window shade was pulled down allowing only a thin bar of light to enter above the sill and glow in the room's dimness. Sunglasses lay open on the bedside table.

"Hi Bobby."

On the bed lying on his back with one hand open was the same bald big man, his face turned towards me with opaque eyes that peered out of an expressionless face. There was an absence of himself in his look that I was unprepared for. Hard to imagine that he couldn't yet throw back the covers and leap out of bed, his lips pinched in anger and his right fist cocked to sweep across with a hook that had dropped a couple of men in the stores' backroom. But the way his covers were tucked in around his body belied that possibility and suggested instead a small child who accepted whatever his mother put on him.

"How are you doing, Dad?"

"Better. . . . The headaches are gone."

His words emerged carefully framed. They sounded machine made.

"They gave him steroids and they're helping," Mother said from the foot of the bed.

"Ask me . . . who said what."

He'd forgotten the word "quotation" and was making do with "who said what."

"He wants to test himself," Mother explained.

Dad had books of quotations at home and used them generously in his speeches. I tried to think of one he knew well . . .

"How about, 'Lafayette, we are here.' "

"That was General George Pershing . . . that the Yanks are here. . . . Ask me another. . . ."

He wasn't just testing himself, I suspected. He was competing, no longer with Kroger and A. and P., but with that part of his brain in thrall of the tumor. Dad wasn't yielding good brain cells without a fight. It was no different from when Dr. Chambers told him to either take up golf or drop dead from cardiac arrest. When I joined him at Shoreacres Golf Course, he coughed loudly during Uncle Jack's back swing, stepped on Uncle Jack's ball on the fairway and kicked his own ball nearer the hole when he thought no one was looking. Now, before I could come up with another quotation he became his own interrogator.

"Who said, 'The only thing we have to fear is fear itself?' That was Franklin Delano Roosevelt.... And who said ... Patrick Henry he said ... It was Patrick Henry who said ..."

"The steroids are interfering with your thinking," Mother said to him. "That's enough."

"What did we run, Bobby, in the ad?"

"Do you want me to get a newspaper?" I asked him.

"I want.... Promise me you'll get in the business."

What?! ... Where had *that* come from? He said he'd never ask again. Had he lost the last five years? Or did he still have it to be crafty on his deathbed? My hand was in his. What did he expect me to say? I could lie. Or say nothing. He might forget he asked....

I glanced at Mother but her look was far away. She was plump in a Levantine way with a thin beaked nose and large, soulful eyes. There was no gray in her red-brown hair. Time hadn't yet dimmed the august glamour in her face. She looked forty-nine, the age she passed herself off as. I could imagine her quoting with the greatest sincerity from Oscar Wilde, "You know, Bobby, giving one's correct age sounds so calculating."

She couldn't have heard Dad's request or I'd be hearing the usual tirade.

"How can you refuse him? For whom has he been working eighty hours a week for all his life? *Achwheat!* (Crazy)," she'd tell me in Arabic. "Thirty-six supermarkets, the largest shopping centers ... Your cousins would give their eyeteeth to be where you are."

My cousins could have the business. I'd been crazy since before I had eyeteeth, since Grandfather's second wife and the baby died in childbirth. Then, my life changed. "Your grandfather's lonesome," Dad told us, "so we're going to live with him." It was 1941. I was five and my brother Ted was four when we moved into Grandfather's Woodlawn house, a baronial gothic mansion with carved heads in the corners of the ceiling, a hidden bar in the basement and a fountain room. Ted and I stayed with our nanny, Mrs. Post, in the maid's quarters behind the kitchen because Grandfather, who founded and controlled Hamady Bros., conducted formal business and entertained in the front rooms. We weren't to venture out unless we were summoned. We'd hear talking and laughter, and then Dad would come back and tell us to stand up straight so he could tuck in our shirts, tie our shoelaces, and push the hair off our foreheads. After that came our instructions.

"Now listen to me. I want you to go out there and be perfect gentlemen. Go first to your grandfather—Hello *Zhidee*— and kiss him on the cheek. Then go round and shake hands with everyone. You know some of them—Mr. Workus, Uncle Sol. When you sit down I want you to sit up straight, don't whisper, don't fidget, don't pick your nose. Remember, your grandfather is going to be looking at you to see if you measure up, and if he has doubts, he might sell the business. When

Flint Delegates in W

U. S. Far Ahead in Prosperity, Michael Hamady Says on Return to Flint With Bride From Syria

Recession or no recession, the United States still is the most prosperous place in the world.

Just returned from Syria — where, in his old home town, he took a bride — Michael Hamady had that to report today as he prepared to swing back into business affairs after his first extended vacation in many years.

Mr. Hamady, president of Hamady Brothers, was in Italy twice and traveled widely in Syria during the journey that began here June 6 and ended Saturday when he arrived with his wife, Sauada, at his home at 6315 Branch road.

He found, he said, that financial conditions were poor both in Italy and the Near East. There was "no comparison whatever," he said, between the degree of prosperity prevailing in America and that he observed abroad.

Syrians Like F. R.

"The American people should consider themselves fortunate," he went on. "Those who are not satisfied — let them travel through Europe and the eastern countries and they will be convinced the old U. S. A. is the greatest place in the world.

"There's only one place for me— that's America."

Mr. and Mrs. Hamady left Syria Oct. 6, soon after the four-power accord had removed the threat of a general European war. Mr. Hamady recalled that President Roosevelt's plea to Hitler for continuance of negotiations had made Syria "very happy."

"The people worshiped America and Roosevelt after the President made his suggestions," Mr. Hamady said. "Those people have had enough trouble since the World war. They don't want any more."

Mr. Hamady did not go to Palestine and expressed no views on the strife between the Jews and the Arabs. "You hear one story and then the other," he said. Nothing out of the ordinary befel him during his travels in Syria, he declared.

Married Aug. 7

A native of the Lebanese town of Baaklin, Mr. Hamady was married there Aug. 7. Baaklin also was the home of Mrs. Hamady whose surname was the same as the merchant's. He said that she was a distant relative, and he had known her and her parents for years.

Merchant Returns With Bride — Michael Hamady president of Hamady Brothers, returned to Flint Saturday from a trip to Syria, where on Aug. 7, in his native Lebanese town of Baaklin, he married Sauada Hamady. The picture of the bride and bridegroom was taken in Syria.

Mr. Hamady crossed the Atlantic on an Italian liner and landed in Naples. He stayed there a short time and then went on to Alexandria, Egypt, whence he journeyed to Beirut, Syria. On the retun, he and his wife sailed from Naples, and there were stops at Genoa and Gibraltar.

There were many relatives and friends with whom to renew acquaintance in Syria. Mr. Hamady had not been there since 1920. He came to the United States at the age of 24, in 1909, lived in Caro for a year and then entered business in Flint, where 10 Hamady markets are now in operation. Mrs. Hamady saw America for the first time when she came here with her husband.

The Woodlawn house

you're asked what you're going to be when you grow up I want you to look him straight in the eye and say—'We're going to be grocerymen, Grandfather.' And this time, look like you mean it."

We marched out with Dad in the rear, past the kitchen and under the circular staircase, into the hall with a giant cathedral lantern hanging on a chain from the third floor. Dad's hands would come down on our shoulders as we turned and entered the long rectangular living room with French doors on each side. After being in the small rooms and plain walls of the maid's quarters, the living room was rich with the coral, ivory and blue colors of the long Kerman rug, the pale gold and silver petit point scenes on the French chairs, and the gilded frames on oil paintings of the Cornish coast and tethered stallions rearing before a stable boy. At the far end of the living room, visible through filigree iron doors, was the fountain room with a frieze of a woman that had been nude until Grandfather commissioned a sculptor to clothe it. Grandfather was always in his chair near the entrance with his back to us. He sat erect, dignified, a well dressed and handsome man with white hair below his bald head, and dark eyebrows.

"Hello, *Zhidee*," we said in our huskiest voices.

"Hello, Grandsons" he hailed back without turning, smiling at his guests as he received his kisses.

"These are my grandsons," he declared to everyone.

"This is the third generation, huh, Mike," someone would say. "Shirt sleeves to shirt sleeves?"

"Shirt sleeves to shirt sleeves," Grandfather would repeat.

"Shirt sleeves to shirt sleeves," Dad echoed with a nervous laugh.

After shaking everyone's hand we sat with straight backs and practiced solemnity on the designated love seat facing Grandfather. The conversation would then be directed at us while Grandfather listened, amused, watchful of our expressions.

Uncle Sol, a "cousin" whose common ancestor with Grandfather might have been Phoenician, would start. He'd spent fifteen years in the sugar beet fields and he looked a man of the soil, built low and broad with short massive fingers and a full head of black hair that he enjoyed contrasting with Grandfather's bald head.

"Your grandfather and I, we come here and we went up to Caro, up in the Thumb, and we work the beet fields planting and hoeing and picking from sunup to sundown, and when you stood up and broke the horizon line the foreman he'd ride over and point down. And in the winter we lived on rabbit, they lived in the ditches by the hundreds...."

"Was it cold?" Dad asked for our benefit.

Uncle Sol laughed. "One morning Joe Hamady, he my wife's uncle, he went out with a team and wagon to bring back a load of hay, and the temperature dropped to where it was twenty-five below zero. In Lebanon cold is twenty-five above zero, so Joe, he didn't know to get out and walk the horses. And when the team brought the wagon back Joe was still in the wagon froze to death."

"And you boys listen to this," Dad said. "Your grandfather unloaded a boxcar of coal at night to save enough money to start a grocery store."

Then someone else said, "Your grandfather and Kay when they opened their store they couldn't speak English and they gestured to the customers to just go help themselves and the customers liked it and that was the beginning of selfserve."

Grandfather listened with his eyes twinkling until somebody said, "Your grandfather did all this with a sixth grade education."

"I graduated from the school of hard knocks," he declared.

Everyone laughed. Dad would laugh the hardest. And Ted and I would nod, or look amazed, or seem impressed—whatever reaction was called for. We were doing it for Dad. He wanted his father's love, which he could get through us if we behaved correctly. And we knew it ... we knew it....

How different was Dad from that proud prince, *his* father. He was, in a word, big. One hundred eighty-five pounds of hard frame from wrestling and lifting weights at the old Kearsley Street YMCA, plus the sixty pounds of middle he'd put on within two years of marrying Mother. When he was suited, with his belly ballooning out over his belt and with his bald head shiny from the generous doses of Wildroot hair oil he used to keep the few top hairs in place, he looked more like Grandfather's bodyguard than his son. He never wore a sports jacket as Grandfather always did. And he didn't have Grandfather's love of flowers and gardening, Arabian horses and a beautiful setting. In short, he lacked Grandfather's elegance. I watched him dancing once, leading Mother through the box step he'd been pressured into learning at Arthur Murray Dance Studio. His lips were moving with the count, his suit pants didn't make it down to his shoes and his socks didn't make it up past his ankles. And I felt, there's the real hero out there, not Grandfather. Because heroes are big and fat and wholesome and smell of produce. Because heroes come back from deer hunting up North and rub their unshaven cheek against the side of your face. And because I loved him.

"So, Mike, you knew early on that you wanted to start a business," someone said. "What made you pick the grocery business?"

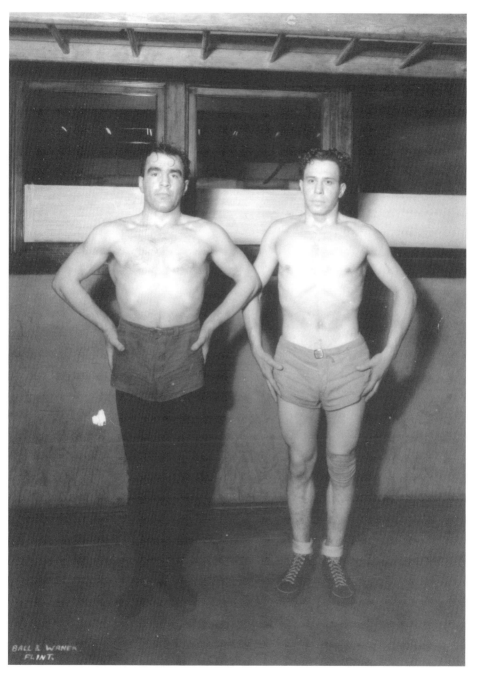

Dad and wrestling opponent at the YMCA, 1933?

Hamady Bros. Food Stores Marking 40th Anniversary

Accordingly, all Hamady stores were built with parking lots easily accessible to the stores, which were put on a self-serve basis.

Mr. Hamady designed much of the equipment and furnishings used in the stores and laid down many of the practices and policies which have helped make the firm the largest single retail food outlet in Flint.

He designed many of the decorative patterns in tile that are a hallmark of the Hamady stores. Most Hamady stores have ceramic tile on the walls to a height of about 10 feet. Colors are rose, buff and black, with brown figuring.

As the business grew, each Hamady store incorporated the most advanced sanitation ideas, including germicidal lamps which prevent growth of bacteria on meats.

The firm used warehouse facilities at 161 Lewis St. before 1942, when it moved to 501 W. Kearsley St. But the growing firm found both places too small, and built the modern warehouse and supermarket on Dort. Hwy. near Atherton Rd., which was completed in July, 1949.

The warehouse there handles in excess of 100 tons of food a day for the Hamady stores. The building, including store and warehouse, measures 650x180 and is among the largest grocery establishments in the State.

Top executives of food-processing firms are expected in Flint to give congratulations to the firm.

FORTIETH ANNIVERSARY—Executives of Hamady Bros. look over an early run of the 48-page section of full page advertisements appearing in today's Journal marking the 40th anniversary of the grocery firm. Seated is Michael Hamady, president and founder. Standing (from the left) are Robert M. Hamady, secretary-treasurer; L. W. Lambertson, second vice-president; K. C. Hamady, first vice-president, and Jack A. Hamady, third vice-president. (Journal Photo)

One of the pages was contributed by Hamady employees as an anniversary present.

Planning for the ads began in June and the first "copy" was received Sept. 5. The section was printed Wednesday and inserted into today's paper.

The first Hamady store was established by Michael Hamady at Dayton St. and Industrial Ave. in 1911 and was no longer than some of the display counters used in the chain's modern super markets. Now the firm's 13 stores have more than five acres of floor space and about 600 employees.

Mr. Hamady still is president and active although he leaves direct operations to others. The other officers: First Vice-President, K. C. Hamady; second vice-president, L. W. Lambertson; third vice-president, Jack A. Hamady, and secretary-treasurer, Robert M. Hamady.

Michael Hamady pioneered automobile food shopping here. He was convinced that the successful food retailer must provide automobile parking and lots of

Firm's 49 Pages of Advertising Set Record for Any Newspaper

First Store Established at Industrial Ave. And E. Dayton Street in 1911

Forty-nine full-page advertisements in today's Journal mark the 40th anniversary of Hamady Brothers, Flint's largest locally-owned food stores and among the nation's best known.

According to available information, this is the largest number of pages ever published by a single firm in any single edition of any newspaper.

The ads take up almost 9,000 column inches. The type alone for the 49 pages weighed 2½ tons and engravers made 500 plates. Forty-eight of the pages will run together in one section and the other is a "teaser page" in another section.

Dad answered, "I'll tell you why. Because with a rented room and a carton of Kellogg's Corn Flakes, you were in business. That's all your grandfather had to sell when he opened his first store across from the Buick factory."

"And, Mike, you knew you wanted to start in Flint," Mr. Workus said. He was the General Motors vice president who got Grandfather his Buicks, Dad told us.

Grandfather spoke, looking directly at us. "It didn't take a genius to see that automobiles were the coming thing. Bay City had the location on Lake Huron but they were complacent, content to sit on their laurels. And they didn't want the immigrants and laborers that came with the factories. Flint did. Flint had nothing going for it except ambition and it went out and brought in Buick and Chevrolet and became a boomtown. And look at Bay City today. It's where we go to fish for perch."

Everyone laughed again. And Ted and I joined in, knowing that *we* were Bay City, self-satisfied and unambitious.

"Robert," someone said, "can you imagine if your father can build a Hamady Bros. with a sixth grade education, what Bob and Ted here will accomplish with a college education?"

"You can't learn it in school," Grandfather said. That was followed by silence.

"Too much education, it makes a man soft, makes him so he doesn't want to work, and then he starts looking for shortcuts to success...."

Behind Grandfather, Dad's expression was telling us to get ready. And when Grandfather said, "Maybe when my grandsons grow up and become educated they'll turn their backs on the business...."

Dad spoke out. "All right, let's hear it from those grandsons. What are you boys going to be when you grow up?"

"WE'RE GOING TO BE GROCERYMEN, GRANDFATHER!" we shouted.

Grandfather smiled around at his guests. But he wasn't done.

"A man starts a company. To get business he knows he has to please the customer. So he gives better service than his competition and better quality and he cuts his prices. And his customers are happy and the business grows. And then his son comes into the business and he carries on his father's philosophy of first pleasing the customer, and the business continues to expand. Then *his* sons come into the business and they say—why are we spending so much money on such a large selection of goods. So they cut back. And they say—we can save money on help. So they cut back on service. And they keep finding this way and that to save money. But their competitors are hungry for business and pretty soon they're taking away the customers. And sales go down. And then, one day, that business is out of business ...

"... A business can last only three generations. First generation founds the business. Second generation builds the business. Third generation brings it down."

A hush followed, as if a passage had been read from the Bible. Something momentous had been proclaimed. Hamady Bros., the celestial family business, would be betrayed. Not deliberately, but inevitably, through ineptitude and sloth. Its doom was ordained ...

... *if* we went into the business.

Grandfather Mahmoud, 1905?

Grandfather Mike, 1914?

Joe, Kay and Mike, *The Hamady Bros.* in a joke photo sent to Baakleen, 1919?

Hamady Bros. grand opening, 1928?

II

Twenty years later as I was graduating from law school, I took myself to see the resident psychiatrist at the University of Michigan health service, Dr. Kimbrough, a big man in his thirties with groomed premature white hair. Don't want to get into the family business, I told him. Went to law school to avoid it but now I'm graduating.

"Why come to me?" he asked. "That's not a psychiatric problem."

The business wasn't. But Dad was. I had a conflict. Dad's life, his happiness, depended on *me*. If I rejected the business I'd hurt him. That's what I believed. He was vulnerable. I'd always felt sorry for him, because of his needs, because of his life. Grandfather left for America when Dad was three months old. Eleven years later Grandfather returned, divorced Dad's mother and brought Dad and his brother Louie to America. And Grandfather forbid them from writing to their mother. It would be fifteen years before Dad saw her again. Louie never would. Then, when Grandfather went bankrupt in 1923 he pulled Dad and Louie out of school in the tenth grade and put them to work rebuilding the business. They had to work hard. From all accounts Grandfather was an unforgiving man. In 1928 Louie killed himself with a shotgun. Dad swore it was an accident. But was it? Dad had survived but he suffered. And I became his protector.

"Are you still?" the psychiatrist asked.

I was. Love is care, Dad liked to say. I cared for Dad. But it was the business he cared for. Hamady Bros. was his favored child. Grandfather had an offer—a good offer—to sell the business in 1957. Dad begged him not to. "What if you died?" Grandfather asked, because Dad was running it then, still as a one-man business. Dad offered to insure his own life for $10,000,000 and make Grandfather the beneficiary. Grandfather didn't sell. Thereafter, whenever there was a rumor that the business was for sale, Dad would hunt down the source and threaten him with litigation, or worse.

I knew Dad's grief when he had been severed from his mother. I imagined that Dad saw himself as the business and that he became his mother to it. Then, fearing his father might again separate them Dad had to convince him that the two grandsons were dying to come in to perpetuate the business. My role became clear. I dressed in a suit or in my military school uniform so Dad could parade me around in the stores. I gave everyone a smart handshake and a confident smile, and I spoke to Grandfather and his courtiers like a future groceryman—though I'd never be one—while looking them squarely in the eye. I knew that if I did gravitate into the business I'd be made a vice president and director and be where any twenty-five year old would "give his eyeteeth to be." But at what price? I'd continue life as Dad's packaging with no real product inside.

"I don't know who I am."

"Talk about your family," the doctor said.

My family? Well, America may be the land of the individual but I saw myself as a member of a family, the *Hamadys*, an extended family of 50 or 60 members at its peak in 1945, a nation unto itself with its own canon, culture and alliances. The men all came from the same Druze village in the hills of central Lebanon and settled in Flint by way of the sugar beet fields in the thumb of Michigan. Uncle Abraham came first in 1888, and Dad and his brother Louie came last in 1920. In between came three Yousifs who became Uncle Joes, as well as Uncles Selem, Ralph, Kay, Jack, Albert, Frank, Sol, Jim, ...

There were others who returned to the old country or died before I was born. One, a Charlie Hamady, was murdered in a store holdup in 1919. When his murderer was captured and the whereabouts of his detention became known, Charlie's closest relatives went for their guns. Grandfather alerted the police who put Charlie's relatives in jail for a night to cool off. Otherwise, they'd have killed the man. Blood revenge was a family canon.

RULE. YOU PUNISH HIM OR WE WILL.

The family men returned to Lebanon for Druze wives who then married *into* the family. The weekly get-together at one house or another and the annual Fourth of July outing in Flushing Park were family gatherings. In the center of the family, binding everyone closer and illuminating our existence was Hamady Bros., the family business. Grandfather founded it with his cousin Kay, but he was the power. Because of Grandfather there was a Hamady School and Hamady House for the Stepping Stone Girls and Hamady Medical Library. He was the man around whom everyone grouped themselves in the family photographs. He was Mike Hamady, the family patriarch.

My cousins and I, born in Flint, grew up hearing Arabic but speaking only English. Arabic was just a familiar noise, except when it was spoken in anger, as when Mother was looking at my report card after being informed of Cousin Lloyd's good grades.

RULE. SPEAK IN ENGLISH, INSULT IN ARABIC.

"Does your grandfather take a backseat to Uncle Albert? Does your father take a backseat to Uncle Jack? But when we come to you and Cousin Lloyd ... *Ahmar!* (Donkey)."

The music Dad listened or sang along to was the Andrew Sisters or Muhammed Abdul Wahab. Breakfast could be bacon and eggs *bidihin* (with rendered lamb). But fluttering above us all was one flag only: the stars and stripes.

"You felt you were different," Dr. Kimbrough remarked.

"We *were* different. Here's this manufacturing town of a few hundred thousand where practically everyone works for or depends upon General Motors. The aristos making up the country club were local merchants who owed their livelihood to GM, or men with carriage works who'd merged into GM ... men with names like Mott, Dort and Stewart. That's all as it should be. But then you have this cabal of Lebanese Druzes named Hamady who eat raw lamb and speak with accents running the third largest corporation in town after GM and the power company. I had a birthday party where there was Syrian bread (pita) on the table and someone picked it up, examined it, then put his drink on it. When my family went to Lebanon in 1947 the kids in school knew only that we were Arabians returning to an Arabia somewhere."

He smiled.

"By the way," I began, "the Druze ..."

"... Are the warriors of the Levant with a secret religion," he interjected.

I nodded. Dr. Kimbrough couldn't be too astute being a shrink in a university health service. So imagine him knowing *that*.

At the hour's end he suggested I go for an evaluation to a Dr. Jacobs who was *his* analyst and that of some other psychiatrists in Ann Arbor. I shrugged, wrote out a check for fifteen dollars and left.

Strange that I'd have a dream the night before Dr. Jacobs. Actually, it was more like a snapshot. We were on a hill, Steve Wolf and I—he was a friend from military school. And there were sheep around, so we must have been shepherds. That was it.

Dr. Jacobs, fiftyish with a cool, knowing presence, eyed me in silence. I was concerned that the sheep in the dream might denote something sexual, old country style ... "Baa Daady"...

"What color are the sheep?" he finally asked.

I smiled. Yes, some were black. Probably because I didn't want to be a groceryman or I didn't measure up to be one.... Here was I, agonizing about rejecting the business because it would hurt Dad, but he'd willingly sacrifice me to perpetuate it: his memorial. Well, if HE wanted to be Ozymandius—fine!— but I wasn't devoting *my* life to toil on his works. And if I had to dream about black sheep because of it, so be it.

"How would you describe your friend?" Dr. Jacobs asked.

"Steve? Big. Popular. We were defensive tackles on Culver's football team. He said he was going to Depauw—on a football scholarship, he said—which surprised me. I didn't consider him that good."

"Could he have been making it up?"

"I thought so. But he did look the part—big, immovable seeming. He looked better than what he was, like those Marlboro men in the ads, those fairies with rugged faces, those phonies. I think Steve bought into his looks. I don't think he knew who he was ..."

I broke off to consider what I'd just said, to marvel at the coincidence.

"... You know, that's what I said about myself."

"You've been describing yourself," Dr. Jacobs said.

That had me backtracking, recalling my description of Steve.

"I'm not saying Steve was a fruitcake!"

"A fairy with rugged features," Dr. Jacobs read from his note pad.

I only meant that he appeared to be somebody he wasn't. But what did that make me? What lurked under *this* façade? What *was* the façade?

The session ended with my identity unresolved and my mind in turmoil. I left for Red's Rite Spot and a smoke. When my coffee came I lit up a ... Marlboro. I took a drag as Grandfather's living room played out in my mind—the long Kerman rug, the French doors, the fountain room, *the grand piano*—I'd forgotten—and above it, the large Victorian painting of a foppish boy with long black locks in red velvet and lace, leaning easily against an ebony stand.

"That's who I thought I was!" I exclaimed to Dr. Kimbrough at our next hour. "Blue Boy. A fop. A mama's boy. A pretty boy. That's me. And I'd grow up to be a playboy."

"A boy," said Dr. Kimbrough. "Not a man."

"No. You've got to be self-made to be a man. And Ted and I can never be that. 'For *we* on honey-dew hath fed and drunk the milk of Paradise.' "

I was silent, feeling the familiar distaste and repellence of myself that now had been given visible form. There was a sense of being illegitimate, unwholesome, pretty, a groomed doll to be passed around by adoring mothers in a cushioned parlor while their husbands were away waging economic war.

"Is there anyone more insufferable than a self-made man?" I heard Dr. Kimbrough ask.

I smiled before I realized why. After all the glorification of Grandfather that made me feel like a fop by comparison, here was someone—a psychiatrist!—saying the great man was a pain in the ass. If only Dr. Kimbrough had been in Grandfather's living room to whisper that *then*, when we were isolated and without a single ally. Insufferable! Oh, that was perfect. I had heard Mother call him that but I'd discounted it because those two had run-ins, both having claims on Dad, and poor Dad caught in the middle. She might have called him that to his face, which would explain why Grandfather kicked Cousin Ernie's products out of the store; Ernie having the misfortune to be her brother-in-law. Grandfather might be insufferable but he was still the king.

When the session ended, Dr. Kimbrough asked if I wanted to continue meeting once a week or twice. He was in private practice now and had raised his fee to twenty-five dollars. The timing narrowed my one eye, but I said nothing for fear of appearing hydraheaded in his diagnosis. What was my diagnosis anyway? I wondered. He couldn't say because I hadn't talked yet about Mother. So, I elected to come twice a week. We'd been mining for lead in a gold mine.

Michigan Druze, Grandfather center, Louie and Robert front left and right, 1921

A friend, Grandfather, Dad, and Uncle Frank, 1934.

Grandfather with Lily, Millie and Hajar, 1935

Dad with me and Ted, right, 1939

Family outing, me and Ted front row left, 1944?

III

Most people regard food as something to put into the body. Mother saw food as something to put *through* the body. So, rather than seeing it as destined for the stomach she pictured it on its way to the toilet. The difference appears semantical but the pain that resulted cannot be exaggerated.

At issue was cleanliness. To her, excrement was something that food evolved into after a time period, whether or not it had been expelled. And, she asked, if excrement is dirty outside the body, can it be clean inside it? Since cleanliness was next to Godliness, retention was the devil. She would defeat the scourge ... with the purge.

Her first attempt to give me an enema was in 1941, about the time of Pearl Harbor. It was a disaster because I was too young to hold it. She would wait until 1944 when I was eight. Eight was when a boy became a man, sphincter-wise.

By then we'd moved out of the Woodlawn house. Mother gave as the reason that she wanted a more normal life for Ted and me, away from Grandfather and life at Versailles. Years later Cousin Roy would intimate that Mother had had one too many run-ins with the Sun King.

We moved into a brick and tile roof house in a pleasant but not ritzy neighborhood of doctors and local businessmen, and we exchanged our nanny nurse for a housekeeper. Cook Elementary School, a square red brick building set down between two playing fields, one for baseball and the other for kick the can, was just across the boulevard. In front of our house was

At Grandfather's cottage on Mackinac Island, 1946

a small park, and up the street a hill for sledding down in winter. Kittycorner was Eli's grocery whose door opening bell would send Eli downstairs muttering curses at having to sell me a penny pretzel stick. On nearby Detroit Street were two drugstores where we could sit with sodas and read comic books after school. The Della Theater with its Saturday matinee of reruns and serials was five minutes in the other direction, running all the way.

Mother was soon putting up peaches and strawberries, and grape leaves collected from the park across the street, storing them near where Dad kept and cleaned his guns. He now had a study. Ted and I shared the den with old Mrs. Grady, our housekeeper. The living room, even with slip covers, was off limits, but after the Bastille on Woodlawn, who cared?

There was only one problem with all that life now had to offer. Mother. We weren't allowed to cross a street by ourselves. Mr. Peabody who directed traffic at the school crossing had to come over and walk us across—only us. In Winter when everyone else wore earmuffs and jackets, corduroy pants and rubbers, we had to wear parkas, leggins, galoshes, and a leather helmet cap with flaps that left only the eyes exposed. If our tongue was coated or on Mother's whim or off mood, we couldn't go outside to play.

Ted and I might look to Dad to rescue us but those hopes had been dashed one day at the Woodlawn house. Dad had wanted to take us to select a pumpkin for Halloween. Mother said no for some obscure health reason. Dad hollered at her and stormed about, bucking and kicking a chair away and smashing his mandolin against the wall. But we didn't go. He made up an excuse and we didn't go. My father, so physically formidable and so in the right, had been broken. How to make sense of it? I was confused, and furious at Mother. Ted saw what I saw and shrugged: what can you do? I asked myself the same question ... but not with a shrug.

My fear of another enema came on a hot summer afternoon in 1944. It must have been Saturday because Dad was in the den in his easy chair reading the Flint Journal. Ted and I were on the floor playing Chinese Checkers. We were brothers with no resemblance. He was quiet and focused. I was neither. "Thank God for your brother!" Mother said to me more than once. Then, too, he was light complected and freckled with curly brown hair. I was darker with straight black hair. "Put your hand against mine," Dad had asked once and I did. "You see the same fingers, the same flat nails? Your brother, God bless him, he's from your mother's side. But you take from me."

Everything was fine that day until Mother materialized in the doorway with a dishtowel and surveyed our scene.

"You haven't gone today."

That's how it began. She had no respect for my privacy and I hated her for it.

"So?" I answered.

"So, why don't you go in and try."

"I can't go."

"How do you know without trying?"

"I don't need to try. I can tell."

"Robert?" she called out to enlist Dad's help.

"Bobby, why don't you go in and try," he said from behind his newspaper, "What do you have to lose?"

"I'm not going and that's that!"

"Millie, let it go," Dad said, turning a page. "When he can go he'll go."

"Its been two whole days!" she told him. "How long are we supposed to wait? How long do you wait when your produce managers don't produce?"

Dad took his newspaper and retreated upstairs. When the bathroom door slammed, Mother said,

"See what you do when you hold back?"

Dad didn't come down until dinner was called. By then he had a feedbag joviality. He started in with a big spoon on the bowl of Arabic rice and garbanzos Mother made for him.

"Millie, consider yourself kissed on both cheeks."

He winked to show how enjoyable eating could be. I had speculated once on the probable size of *his* stools and decided I wouldn't have bet against him in a bout with a bear.

"You better eat if you want to make a stool," Mother told me.

How could I bring a friend home for dinner if she might erupt with that?! And the food she laid out, at least the American food, had her stamp on it: nourishing and inedible. That night the pot roast was way overcooked and dry. One bite and I plunged my fork into the meat and folded my arms. Dad said not to throw it out but to take it for Major, our neighbor's English pointer.

Mother said, laughing, "Tonight we'll give it to Major and tomorrow he'll give it back to us."

We liked it when Mother laughed. And she did take the food for Major. When she was gone I heard Dad go back into the refrigerator. Mother returned and she heard it too because she started hollering at him.

"Robert, no more. You've had enough. Give me that grapefruit. Look at you. You don't know when to stop. Give it to me ..."

When I charged into the kitchen he was holding the grapefruit aloft good naturedly and fending her off.

"Leave him alone!" I said, tugging on her arm.

"Bobby, your mother's right" he said and brought the grapefruit down.

"I don't care. You can eat what you want. She can't treat you like that."

"Do you want your father to eat himself into the grave?" she said, which made me hug Dad.

"My son, my son," he said, patting my back.

"*Dahlic, int!* (Spare me)," Mother said to him, "If he's such a chip off the old block, let him go to the bathroom and show it."

Then, as she started up the stairs, "As for you, you've got until ten o'clock tomorrow."

I had no doubt what she meant and I pulled on Dad's shirt sleeve. "I'm not having an enema!"

"Who said anything about an enema?" he told me. "You're going to go. You just need a night to digest your food."

"What if I can't?"

"You will, take my word for it."

When he saw I wasn't, he raised his hand solemnly. "*Wha -yat Allah*. You're going to go, and there will be no enema. Honest to God. Okay?"

I stared at him. Was he my ally, like I was his? . . .

"There's an old Druze legend," he once told Ted and me, "about a man from one clan that married a woman from another clan, and they went to live with his family. And they had a son. One day war broke out between the two clans, and in the middle of one night the mother took the baby from his crib and went back to her family. And there the baby grew up into a young man. One day he rode into battle against his father's clan, and he came face-to-face with the man he knew to be his father. 'Before you strike,' his father called out, 'ask yourself: whose son am I?' … The young man thought. Then he turned his horse to fight alongside his father."

I knew whose son I was. But with whom was his loyalty?

"Be optimistic," he advised now. "How did George Washington with a puny militia defeat the strongest army in the world? Tonight before you go to bed you tell yourself—tomorrow morning when I wake up, by God, I'll show her. Okay? Now go up and listen to the radio with your brother."

The radio referred to was yellow plastic with a circular dial that sat on the table between our beds. We listened to *Suspense* and *Death Valley Days* until 9:00, which was lights out and too early to sleep, then we turned the volume way down and listened on to *Major Bowles Amateur Hour*. Mother would send Dad, weighing 245 pounds, to creep up the stairs and listen, so when we heard the stairs creak we turned it off and pretended to sleep. Sometimes he came in and, after feeling that the radio was warm, stood there for a half minute or so until one of us had to laugh. Eventually, Ted was moved into the guest bedroom.

Later that night I lay on my bed in the dark and listened to the locusts out the open window and, at times, the dull iron clunk and reverberation of boxcars coupling and uncoupling down on Water Street … and I imagined climbing out the window and swinging down from the roof and running the fourteen blocks to Water Street and hopping up into a boxcar to be with the hobos staggering back from Reese Jones Bar, then watching Flint and Mother sliding away out of my life, away, away, away …

Next morning I rose and went into the bathroom and what I produced was worse than nothing. With nothing there was still the potential. Better to sell Mother the sizzle than the steak when it looked like this. I flushed it away.

When I came downstairs she gave me a tall glass of milk of magnesia to drink which tasted like liquid chalk. I finished it and my face in the mirror looked like a Kabuki mask. Mother said that if the laxative was going to work I had to relax and not fight it. She had me sit beside her on the sofa. On her lap was a Mary Lee candy box.

"I thought we could look at stamps together," she said.

Inside the box were air mail letters from Aunt Affifi in Buenos Aires and Uncle Hassan in Dakar and from the Ivory Coast and Egypt and Syria and Belgium and Brazil, letters covered with stamps of faces and flowers and birds and ruins with interesting postmarks and Arabic written in the margins. As her fingers shuffled through the envelopes she bent her head closer, pausing now and then to examine one and, I thought, to remember. There was one packet of letters bound with a green ribbon and when I reached for it she pushed my hand away.

"They're from your father and they're in English and they're private," she said.

Then she began to tell how it was when Dad came to call, and how there had been previous suitors because her father, Abbas Salha, was the Druze leader of his town. He'd gone to Brazil and made money in gold someway and came back and brought electricity to his village and built the big house on the hill.

I listened as she told of the standing her father enjoyed, the servants that spoiled her, the leisure of afternoon tea on the patio while her brothers looked for things to shoot in the distance, and her friends at boarding school in Beirut. She was

Mother and friend Hilda, 1931?

Grandfather Abbas and children, 1933?

Dad and Mother set to leave for America, 1935

Newlyweds with the *family*, 1935

Lebanese, really, not American like Dad; an odalisque out of a painting by Matisse, smelling faintly of Shalimar, which I'd learned to distinguish from the Chanel Number Five on her dressing table. There was no scent of the produce house on *her*, no dirt under her nails, no history and glorification of struggle. I listened, and was drawn in.

She said that Dad came to visit with a Doctor Hamady from the High Hamadys, whatever that meant. And that he'd forgotten Arabic except for certain phrases that one can't do without, like "Thank you, I've eaten enough." He was athletic looking and direct and he smiled. He was an American, she said, except that he had a Kemal Attaturk mustache. What kind, I asked? Like Hitler's she said, and we laughed.

"One of your father's relatives in Flint," she explained, "from his village of Baakleen—those people are old fashioned, you know—he probably told Robert that it was the fashion, and your father living in Flint and all the time working, what did he know?"

I liked that she was confiding in me. She told of marrying Dad with great expectations of the life she would lead, then finding herself in a dreary manufacturing town with an overbearing father-in-law and an absentee husband. I felt sorry for her. I knew her afternoons now were spent on the sofa with a bag of caramels rereading Screenguild Magazine, from which she might look up to inform me, "While Keenan Wynn was away in the service, Van Johnson stole his girl friend. His best friend!" In the background a tango played on the phonograph.

She asked me to go to the bathroom and try. I went though I knew the outcome. When I came out and shook my head, I saw her mentally cross *laxative* off her list.

Sunday breakfast was always waffles but I wasn't hungry. Mother never made the connection between eating and bowels.

She didn't figure that if I don't eat there's nothing to retain. She reasoned back from the desired result: if I didn't go *it* must still be in there. That morning no one was talking about my predicament. Ted wasn't affected so he was indifferent, like the wildebeest that had escaped the lions charge and was back grazing within sight of where his brother was being devoured. I was still calling the pita Syrian bread and had to be corrected. France had recently carved Lebanon out of Syria, creating a new country, and the bread on our table was now Lebanese bread.

After breakfast Dad asked me to follow him into his small study off the living room. His desk faced a wall of books so he turned his desk chair to face me on the sofa, then waited to let the tension build while his electric desk clock whirred behind him. How terrible it was to be taken from your mother, he began. How lucky I was to have a mother who cares.

"Love is care, Bobby," he intoned.

I saw what was coming and I didn't like it.

"You promised!"

"Wait one minute," he said. "I'm a man of my word. Just hear me out."

What choice did I have?

"You know that we are Druze," he began. "And you know there aren't many of us in the world. We've survived a thousand years. Why? Because we are united. Any Druze in trouble who needs aid can ride into any Druze village and say, *Kam baroodi*—How many guns?—and the whole village will come out to help him. Well, son, that's what I'm saying to you now. Kam baroodi. I need your help. Just this once. I know you don't understand now. Someday you will when you're married. I know I'm asking a lot. Are you going to come to my aid? What is my son's answer? …"

I searched Dad's expression for a way out. Hope gave way to hopelessness.

"You're a good boy," he said and kissed my cheek. "I'm proud of you. You're a GOOD BOY. It'll be over in no time, you'll see. Go on outside now but stay around and I'll whistle when its ready."

I stepped outside and slumped ... then started walking up the block.

Soon I was noticing the blue stars hanging in the windows that spoke of a son or husband in the war. I knew which neighbors had them. The houses with gold stars, the ones that had received a telegram that began "We regret to inform you," I'd see on our evening ride with Dad to tend our victory garden on Mackin Road. From the family, Cousin Ernie was in a tank somewhere in France, Roy was in England, Bill was in India, Fred and Big Joe were somewhere, and Little Joe was a marine in the Pacific. "Shoo shoo shoo baby goodby goodby, your papa's off to the seven seas," the Andrews Sisters were singing on radios everywhere. And on the home front Ted and I saved the tin foil from our gum wrappers, went on paper drives, searched the skies for Japanese Bettys and Carolines, and listened with Dad as the radio recounted the allied and enemy planes downed. Dad had joined the State Troops after Pearl Harbor but then was discharged to direct the food rationing program in Flint.

I stopped walking and was looking down. On the treelawn was the turd that Major had processed from my left-over pot roast. There it was! Just what Mother was hoping for. And then some. My heartbeat quickened as I imagined myself being saved from the electric chair by a last minute appearance of new evidence. I began thinking where I could find a bag, and headed for our garbage can. But when I lifted the lid I visu-

Dad, Kay and Jack, 1943

ized Mother peering down at it in the toilet. And I knew how it would be.

"A minute ago you couldn't go. And now you go *this*?!"

She'd scrutinize me. And then she'd know I hadn't done it. She'd examine the turd, its density, shape, color, size— everything but heft. She'd realize that it was Major's! And that I'd brought it into the house!

I couldn't chance it for the punishment, which would have been unique, no question.

When Dad whistled, I went inside and trudged upstairs to the master bathroom.

Mother was filling the red rubber water bottle from the tap. I took off my clothes and laid down on my back. On the floor beside me was a radio. I watched as Mother hung the water bottle from a hook in the bearing wall and brought down the hose attached to it. When she tested the release above the tub the water came out soapy, like a detergent. Rinso White? She applied Vaseline to the nozzle and worked it in, aided by my grimaces, then sat on the edge of the tub to observe. When the pressure showed on my face she started up a conversation.

"What would you like for dinner?"

"How much more?" I asked.

"Maybe we could have a cookout. Would you like that?"

"How much more?"

"How about hotdogs and baked beans?"

"No more."

"You can help your father with the fire."

"Turn it off, I can't hold it!"

"You better hold it or we'll do it again.... Don't grind your teeth. Move your fingers and toes.... Just a little bit more.... Finished. Very good. What station would you like?"

"GET OUT!"

She put some station on very loud and got out. I pulled myself up onto the toilet and the pressure did the rest. Ten or fifteen minutes must have passed before I felt confident enough to leave. On my bed were clean clothes because now *I* was clean. As I was changing I heard her call up.

"Bobby, hurry up and get downstairs. I made you some lentil soup. You must be starved."

When I described the enema to Dr. Kimbrough, he asked where Dad was during that time. I told him he was probably downstairs reading the paper.

He nodded. "There would be peace in your father's time. You were his Czechoslovakia."

He smiled, expecting me to do the same. When I didn't, he asked,

"There you are, on your back in the female sexual position and your mother is sticking a hose in you. How did that make you feel?"

I stared back, silent, sullen.

"Where's your father?" he asked. "What is he letting Mother do to you?"

"What are you trying to get me to feel?!" I said sharply.

"What *do* you feel? What are you feeling now? ... Where's the RAGE?! . ."

I shook my head. It wasn't there.

"You need someone who would bust that door down and say CEASE AND DESIST!" he said. "Someone to identify with who would stand up to Mother. Who would that be?"

The answer came easily. "Grandfather."

Dr. Kimbrough arched his eyebrows.

"Why would he bother?" I said, scowling. "He'd be down-stairs soaking up his accolades. He's too self-concerned to—"

"And your father isn't?"

"At least my father loved me."

"And Neville Chamberlain loved Prague."

That penetrated my defense of Dad. Love is care, isn't it? Downstairs reading the paper while Mother pumped in the pain, it was himself Dad was caring about.

"Talk to your grandfather," he said. "Spend time with him. Look past the icon you grew up with. Try to connect with the man. He's not a saint but you need him. 'Paris is worth the Mass.' "

IV

Mid October, 1961: I was 25, and took a day off from studying for the Michigan Bar to pheasant hunt with Dad on Valender's farm. There was no hunting politesse with Dad, no "your bird" when one flushed my way. It was root, shoot or die. I told him I was going to visit Grandfather who had just returned to Flint from his cottage on Mackinac Island. "Now you're talking!" he said. "Just remember that law school was just to help you be a better grocery man."

When I arrived at the Woodlawn house the nurse led me into the living room. Grandfather was sitting alone.

"Look who's here," she sang out. "Its your grandson, Robert Lee."

His hands trembled now from Parkinson's, and after we kissed he displayed them for me and shook his head. "Your grandfather has a lot of pride," Dad had told us, "and having his hands shake like that, he's humiliated." Before I could sit he had to look me over and inquire of my height. I'm six one, I said, and he nodded his approval.

"Bring my grandson some coffee and a big piece of that apple pie," he told the nurse. "Bring it all."

"How was Mackinac, Zhidee?" I asked.

"Let me hear you say the Gettysburg Address," he answered and motioned for me to stand.

There was no refusing Grandfather. When the nurse entered with coffee and half a pie, Grandfather gestured for her to stand with the food for my recitation. So, I began, just as I'd

Grandfather, the boss, 1936?

done when I was six and won a hundred dollar savings bond for reciting it at the Masonic Temple; and, repeated it every Lincoln's birthday over the P.A. system at Cook Elementary School. As I was nearing the end . . .

"—that this nation under God shall have a new birth of freedom, and that government of the people, by the people, for the people, shall not perish from the earth."

. . . I was looking directly into his eyes, deep brown and glistening in the lamplight as he gazed up at me, absorbed, his hands trembling freely. It was a strange apparition, the old country autocrat so moved by Abraham Lincoln. One man a rail splitter born in a log cabin the Middle West. The other a stonecutter born in a stone hut in the Middle East. Both self-made men. Dad told us, "Your grandfather never forgets his gratitude for the opportunity this country has given him, and after every dinner on Mackinac Island, everyone—all his guests from Governor Williams to Artie Smyers the office janitor—they all rise and sing God Bless America."

"And now the Declaration of Independence," he called out.

To change the subject, I asked, "Do you remember the names of those seven Arabian horses you had at Mackinac before your heart attack?"

The nurse smiled as he went to work on it.

Grandfather's gratitude wasn't only for his country. I had witnessed it at a dinner in Lansing honoring him as one of the seven grocery pioneers of Michigan, most of whom were Semitic immigrants like himself. "If I could sing," one said in a Russian accent, "I'd sing—There's no business like the grocery business." I saw Grandfather nod and smile, glassyeyed.

"Ebony Idol, Grandson," he exclaimed, smiling. "Do you remember? He'd follow me down the road, no leash, then when we're in front of the Grand Hotel, he knows people are watching and he lifts his head—like that! He's Ebony Idol. He's the prince."

His outstretched hand was shaking wildly and he brought it back and held it against his thigh. The nurse suggested that he was tired and I should leave.

"Nonsense," he said and winked. "I'm going to watch my grandson eat all his pie."

He did. Afterwards, we played a game of gin rummy. Twice in the game when I knocked he played off and undercut me. "What's the matter, Grandson?" his amused expression was asking.

I smiled politely. How was I supposed to identify with such a man, as Dr. Kimbrough had advised. Yes, there was much to admire. He'd gone bankrupt in 1923, lost all ten of his stores. And I'm sure there were some in the family happy to see Mike Hamady get his comeuppance. But he started up again and he paid back his creditors a hundred cents on the dollar despite having no legal obligation to do so.

Did that make me want to identify with him? Not at all. The idea was absurd. And Grandfather would have thought so. "How can you identify with me, Grandson, unless you can pull yourself up by your bootstraps," is what he'd say. There had to be something more than admiration. Grandfather was someone to perform for, to entertain. I didn't love him. But Dad did. And that was all that mattered.

I had wanted to ask Grandfather about Uncle Louie. Dad's story was that his brother had been hospitalized but was released to go for a ride with Uncle Frank. And that Louie asked to stop at the house for something and accidently set off a loaded shotgun kept in the closet. Was it really an accident, I wanted to ask Grandfather. But I didn't dare ...

And no one in the family would tell me. They had conspired to keep each other's secrets.

RULE. "SECRETEZA ET ITERUM SECRETEZA" (SECRECY, THEN MORE SECRECY).

To illustrate: Cousin Karl didn't discover his father had been previously married until his driving instructor mentioned knowing the first wife. She wasn't Druze. Ergo, she was a skeleton ... Another cousin hadn't yet discovered that his father was previously married, to someone sent from the old country who turned out not to be a virgin, and she was sent back. Can't have it bandied around that you'd married used goods ...

So, what hadn't I been told about Uncle Louie? ...

I'd find out without them.

The following afternoon I was in Flint searching through the obituaries in the 1928 Flint Journals. It took awhile but I found it. Louis Michael Hamady. *Accidently* shot himself. He had been hospitalized with *fever of the brain*. What was that? Meningitis? Would they have released him to go out with Uncle Frank if he had meningitis? But for depression ... a ride might raise Louie's spirits, especially if he appeared eager to go ... so he could get at the shotgun he knew was in the closet.

That evening I was at our home on Parkside Drive, the imposing Spanish style house with separate apartments above three mahogany stables that Dad bought for Mother in the mid-fifties. The living room, like Grandfather's, was grand, with a large Kerman rug, French doors and a fountain room, French provincial furniture and a baby grand piano. Dad was amused at my wanting a formal talk in the living room but after a day in the grocery trenches he wanted to know what I had to sell without the small talk.

"What's this all about?" he asked.

"Uncle Louie."

He gestured for me to sit on a small floral sofa and pulled a chair up for himself to face me. When we were seated I found myself sunk down and looking up to where he sat erect, his hands folded, waiting. He'd arranged it deliberately, of course, to dominate. That determined me to get the truth, whatever the cost.

"I found Uncle Louie's obituary."

"And?"

There was no change in Dad's expression. He was not going to open up.

"It was suicide, wasn't it," I said rather than asked.

"What makes you think that?"

"Louie had fever of the brain."

He shrugged. "Louie had *something* but what exactly I don't know."

I had his attention. He was waiting to parry the next thrust.

"I'm 25," I said sharply. "Tell me the truth."

He stared back, silent. He was stalling.

"Why are you protecting your father?" I demanded.

"… You don't know," he began softly, his head shaking. "You don't know … to leave our mother … that dear woman…."

He had one hand covering his eyes. His breathing was stuttered. Never had I seen my father cry. I rose from my chair and put a hand on his shoulder.

"Go back and sit down," he said slowly, coldly and without lifting his head.

When I did, he folded his hands in his lap and regarded me with cool unblinking eyes.

"All right. You want to know why my brother might have been depressed. I'll tell you. When our father left for America I was three months old and Louie was a year older. For eleven years we waited to see our father. We had to wait for the business to succeed. Then we waited for the war to end. Times were hard during the war. The Turkish cavalry commandeered everything. But we were all close. At night we all slept in one big bed, Louie and Mother and I and your Uncle Jack and Aunt Yemna. Finally, there came the Armistice. And then one day my father comes, comes in a Buick, wearing a suit and tie and vest and wearing a Panama hat ... and Mother she still wears the veil...."

His lips were pinched and he paused.

"You don't have to get into all of that," I told him.

"You asked me a question, didn't you?" he asked.

"Yes."

"So now I'm going to answer it. If you have no objections."

There was a mock calm in his tone, inviting me to provoke him, I thought, and then he'd charge out of his chair at me like he'd done when I was twelve and thirteen. He was notifying me that *he* would determine and circumscribe this discussion. When he was satisfied I had no objections, he continued.

"We could see Dad's car coming up the hill because the road has so many switchbacks. When my father drove into Baakleen and got out of his car it was the greatest day of my life. Here was Mother sitting outside on a chair and my brother and I are beside her and the whole village is around us. I'd been waiting all my life to see my father and here he is. The hero of Baakleen, the man I'd only seen in pictures...."

He shook his head. "Somebody brought Dad a pitcher of water—you know, the *brique*—and he held it up and drank without it touching his lips. He wanted to show that he was still *ibn Arab*. But he wasn't. Not anymore. Once we got down to *Wadi Sheik Hassan*—you remember our house, it's a simple house—everything turned sour. I didn't know it but he'd sent Mother money to add another bedroom on to the house and put in a regular kitchen and things like that. And Mother, she's religious and she has the sweetest heart, she gave the money to some of the poor and to the Druze sheiks and she didn't tell Dad. He blew up.

"'Twenty cents of every dollar before the war I sent here,'" he said, "'and for what? So the sheiks can put *hummus* and *jibn* on their table and praise God? Do they think the money comes from God? I'll tell them where it comes from. It comes from the sugar beet fields of Caro, Michigan. Let them go there and earn it. Then on Saturday night when they're paid and their backs are bent and their hands are swollen, then they can praise God.'

"Dad was plenty burned up. And nothing Mother did pleased him. You know how the women are, how they take care of the man.... Have some coffee, some lemonade, some olives and tomatoes, here's a cushion.... He didn't want any of it. I understand *now*. When a man has to start at the very bottom and pull himself up, not knowing the language, with no help from anyone, he comes to resent help. It makes him hard. My father left before I knew him and came back a stranger."

"Your father left when you were three months old," I said. "Then he comes back for the kids. Why did he marry her? Was it an arranged marriage? It sounds like he was looking to get out of there."

"Mother was a religious woman," he said. "For her, God was in Baakleen with her ancestors, and keeping her father alive. God wasn't in America. She had waited eleven years for my father to come back and stay. But Dad was never going to stay. And in the old country, the children go with the father."

I was smirking. "Grandfather knew what he was going to do before he got there. He didn't want to bring back an old country wife who still wore the veil."

He regarded me with a curious expression "... You know, there's something wrong with you. Not your brother. You. I'm sorry to tell you this, but you lack something."

I wasn't put off. "I'm sorry. I'm sorry you had to leave your mother. I'm sorry for everything you had to go through. I'm sorry I didn't go through some of it instead of you. I'm sorry all around. But I still want the truth."

Again, there was that curious expression. "But you think I can tell you the truth without feeling anything?"

His gaze was questioning. I waited.

"... You don't understand. With all your degrees, you don't understand what its like to be caught between your father and your mother, between your father and brother, between this country and the old country,—"

"Between your father and your son," I interrupted.

He appeared stunned.

"... Between my father and my son?" he asked himself slowly, reflectively.

I watched him as he worked to fathom who had the better claim on his loyalty. A son figured to be at the top, as in, "Me and my son against my brother, me and my brother against my cousins," and so on. But so did a father.

"You see Mike Hamady," he asked once after I'd said something irreverent about Grandfather. "He's my father, *right or wrong*. The enemies of my father are my enemies."

I now saw Dad's expression soften. He was amused.

"You want to know the truth about my father? I'll tell you. With him there simply is no middle ground. You're either this or you're that. You're either with him or you can go be whatever you want and God bless you. But you can't be both. That's how he is in business and that's how he was when he brought my brother and me to America. Before we got into that taxi in New York, he got down and kissed the ground. In 1920 Mike Hamady knew who he was. He was an American—not halfway—and he wasn't going to have sons who were half American, who gestured too much and didn't look a man in the eye when they talked and didn't give him a firm handshake and were all the time homesick. So he forbid us to write to our mother until we were Americans. But Mother wrote ... she wrote ..."

He was struggling. I waited.

"... Then when your grandfather went bankrupt in 1923 Louie and I and Jack, we had to quit school in the tenth grade and work. Your grandfather was demanding. His back was to the wall and we worked hard and long. I remember one Sunday we took off from work to go see Tom Mix at a theater and your grandfather found out and he came and pulled us out of there and put us back to work. It got to be too much for Louie separated from our mother and trying to please our father. He left and went to work for a competitor. Krogers, I believe. So, yes, Louie may have been unhappy ... before his accident."

I nodded. For all of Grandfather's character he lacked compassion in equal measure. "You're either my man and take it or your own man and take off." *That* killed Louie. But how is it that one son is dutiful and stays and becomes president of the company and the other is rebellious and takes off and kills himself. I decided not to ask.

"Now, let's talk about you, my son," he said. "I tell people Bob has a degree in business administration and one in law and their eyes get big. So hurry up and graduate. I can use your help in the business. You're Penelope at the loom."

He couldn't let go. And I couldn't tell him. Even if I did, he'd probably be the suitor who dismisses every rejection with, "She'll come around." But I told Dad I'd like to work one day a week to get on the company medical plan because ...

"I'm seeing a psychiatrist."

Predictably he was displeased, and badgered me for my problem. If I said I didn't know who I was he'd think I had amnesia. I kept it in the abstract. And he came around.

"Just don't tell anyone in the family, do you hear? No one. The grandson of Michael Hamady is seeing a head shrinker? *Ya Allah!* If your grandfather found out he'd sell the business. You can come up and work Wednesday afternoons and sign vouchers. You can use Dad's desk in my office. Who knows, you might learn something. Now you better take off before I tell your mother."

RULE. GIVE OUT ONLY GOOD NEWS. BAD NEWS IS MADE GOOD BY HAVING IT WORK OUT FOR THE BEST.

"Bob is fine, never better...."

"He's fortunate. Everyone can benefit by seeing a psychiatrist.

"The needle enters above the eye socket and pokes around the frontal lobe. You should see how reposed he is now. It was a blessing in disguise."

Driving back to Ann Arbor I thought of Dad, so much more tribal than Grandfather, carefully working out his hierarchy of loyalties. In the family pinochle games the sides were always Dad and Uncle Jack against Uncle Kay and Uncle Ralph: first cousins once removed against first cousins. Maybe

Grandfather wasn't tribal, but he knew where he was in the pecking order.

I had read once of the astonishment of Arab sailors a thousand years ago whose vessel happened on a Viking ship in the Mediterranean.

"Who is your leader?" one had called out in a way to make himself understood.

"We have none," was the Viking reply. "We're equals."

Grandfather brings his sons Louie, left, and Robert to America, 1920

Walker School, Louie and Robert second row center, 1922

Robert (Dad) store manager, 1927?

The Patriarch and his lieutenants, Dad and Jack, 1934

Dad reunited with his mother, and his half brother, 1935

V

The following Wednesday I drove to Flint for my half day of gainful employment. Downtown Flint was never pretty but it never put on airs, either. It knew what it was: an overgrown one-horse town, a coach stop on the Detroit to Saginaw road that, like Grandfather, outhustled the competition and made something of itself. Through the forties, going downtown with its department stores and theaters and crowds was an occasion. That was when Flint stopped at the city limits signs. Beyond were croplands and gravel roads and derelict old barns left standing to advertise Redman Chewing Tobacco on their sides.

Then, in the fifties the State Theater and the Strand nearby closed their doors. The advent of television was blamed. But downtown never recovered its old verve and took on a weary and wounded look that I now saw driving down Saginaw Street. Dad didn't care. He'd followed the population moving out with supermarkets and shopping centers and his Northwest Shopping Center could be blamed today for downtown's decline. In fact, Dad privately enjoyed watching the merchants who'd stayed with downtown whine and squirm. Many were Flints' good old boys, the entrenched old money gentlemen with whom Dad was simply out of place.

Until 1947, the Hamady Bros. offices and warehouse were near the downtown and Water Street—aptly named—because the spring thaw that year caused the Flint River to overflow, flooding parts of downtown and resulting in a total loss of merchandise in the Hamady warehouse. The new office and warehouse was built the following year out on Dort Highway near the AC Sparkplug plant. The building was long and rectangular with face brick on all sides, as Dad enjoyed pointing out to visitors. Upstairs above the advertising layout rooms was the reception area where salesmen waited throughout the day for their encounters with the buyers in noisy cubicles crowded with the cans and bottles and boxes of proposed products.

One office only down the hall was private and spacious with a conference table and a second large desk for when Grandfather came. Dad was on the phone when I entered his office and he motioned towards Grandfather's desk and the hundreds upon hundreds of vouchers stacked on it. I sat down and began signing—what, I didn't know. Soon the left hand shuffled as the right hand signed, and I was listening to Dad on his phone call....

"... Are you finished Gus? May I say something? ... Gus? ... Gus? All right, Gus. Now I want to say something. We're doing *you* a favor. We're the customer, Gus, in case you've forgotten. We've been giving and now I'm asking.... Listen, God damn it, I want it and I'll have it or you won't have us.... You don't think so, huh? Listen, is John there? Put him on. Have John come on the line. I want him to hear what I'm going to do...."

The meat manager and the ad layout man appeared at the door and Dad motioned them in.

"... Sure, I'll work with you. Listen, there's some business out there I can steer your way. Don't worry.... Don't worry. Just keep me on your side...."

The meat manager turned to me and winked. "Giving 'em hell."

Dad clowning at a grand opening, 1957.

"... Gus, we all got to eat crow once in awhile. Jesus Christ! I got the government, the unions, the quacks—half my customers are screaming because I'm selling canned hams from Poland and if I stopped.... Tomorrow morning, Gus. Starting tomorrow morning. *Afharisto poli* (Thanks a lot)"

He hung up and made a fist. "We got it! I squeezed Gus and he gave out. Oh, boy, did I enjoy that."

"What would you have done if they called your bluff?" the meat manager asked.

"Bluff! So help me God, if they hadn't come across I'd have shifted the business and taken the loss. Hell, you can't live on crow.... All right, what have you got?"

The meat manager handed him some ad sheets.

"Where's the punch?" Dad asked and pointed at the sheets.

"In the hams and produce."

"Produce, hell! And hams won't carry the ad. Let Krogers run hams and produce. I want to catch them with their pants down. Meat, man, we need meat! What about hamburger?"

"Can't touch it. Frozen boneless is sky high."

"Then run frozen dinners. We'll get a price and run them at cost. Walt, headline it—Mom, take a vacation from the kitchen, or something like that. *Go!*"

They left and Lois opened the secretarial window. "Cyril," she announced.

Dad took the phone. "Cyril? Do you smell any break in the beer price? ... Not even Leo? ..."

I watched Dad's expression shade into resentment.

"... You know something? Those beer distributors have a cozy little deal between them. No one will break price from the others. They're holding up the price and raking in the profits. So here's what we're going to do. Leo is the weak sister among them, the one they'll suspect of caving in to pressure. I want you to build Leo a big display of Carlings Beer and cut the others down to nothing. Maybe they'll think Leo cut a deal with me. Let's see how long they can take him cutting into their share of the market. . . . Yeah, I know its going to cost money but I want to bust up that sweet little cartel they've got. And you watch. One of them is going to break and offer to post a lower price."

He hung up and Lois opened the window, "Charlie McMann."

Still in his hand, the phone returned to his ear. "Charlie? . . . Charlie, what's wrong? . . ."

He leaned back in his chair, listening. A salesman appeared at the door and Dad motioned him to wait.

"Charlie, listen. I'll see what I can do. But don't count on anything do you hear? Nothing."

He hung up and slid open the window. "Get me Ward Baking on the line."

Then, gesturing to me. "Those sons-of-bitches, they're giving Charlie early retirement. Can you beat that! Probably because he works with me. Charlie gives."

He reached down into his bottom desk drawer and brought out a loaf of Syrian bread which he rolled into a tight cylinder. Before he could bite off a piece Lois tapped on the window.

"I want you to hear this," he said to me and pressed the speaker button.

"Bill? How's business?"

"Good, no thanks to you."

"Want to double it?" Dad asked and winked over at me.

"Come on, Robert. No games."

"No games, Bill. Charlie McMann is being given early retirement. Pick him up and he'll get you into the stores. Interested?"

"Sure I'm interested."

"I want the same deal we had with Charlie. I want your cost on white bread and I want cost on buns when we run em. We'll take on a chunk of your bread line and we'll give your cakes a nice display. You'll come out on the cakes.... Bill? ..."

"What do you want me to say? We've been trying to get into your stores for how long? And now ... why are you doing this for him?"

"For me, Bill. If you don't deal with me you're out, Charlie or no Charlie. Business is business. You can work out the details with Cyril. Goodbye."

Dad motioned for the salesman to enter and nodded at me. "How did you like that? That, my son, is POWER!"

Lois opened the window. "There's a Mrs. Czarnecki. I think she wants to complain."

"Czarnecki?" He picked up the phone. "Mrs. Czarnecki, this is Robert Hamady. *Tsi yestes Polkon* (Are you Polish)?"

The salesman cast a puzzled look at me and I turned back to the vouchers. In my mind I heard, "Oh, him. He's the president's older son, works a half day a week. He's a lawyer but he's got a psychiatric problem. Doesn't know who he is. They're letting him sign vouchers. See how he does with that."

After work Dad asked if I would stay for dinner. "She made *kibbee nayee* for you," he said. "She's expecting you. Please, do it for me."

"I don't want to hear Mother's views on the psychiatric profession," I told him.

"Naw, naw, don't worry," he answered and waved me off. "She was concerned when I told her—you know your mother—but I smoothed it over. What you do is your own business. You'll see."

So, I went.

"Well, you don't look like a crazy boy to me," Mother said when she saw me and before we kissed. "What are you telling that psychiatrist? That your parents are these awful people and that they're to blame for everything that's wrong with you?"

"Its not like that, Mother," I said as we sat in the den. "I don't think you're responsible. I think its all genetic."

"And where did you get your genetics?" she said. "Look at your grandfather. And your father. What's wrong with *them*? But when we get to you, you have bad genetics. Silly! Who puts these notions in your head? The psychiatrist? He'll tell you there's something wrong with you so he'll take your money."

"Mother, I don't want to hear anymore about it."

"You don't want to hear the truth. You're going to be brainwashed. He's going to turn you against your own mother and father. You've always been impressionable. You're easily led. You don't have a mind of your own—"

"Shut up!"

Her eyes opened wide in mock astonishment. "Do you want me to tell your father? How you talk to your mother? . . . Apologize this instant!"

". . . Sorry, Mother."

She nodded. You'd better be sorry, her expression said. But I had pleased her by showing that she could still invoke Dad's wrath to control me . . . as she'd done when I was twelve and thirteen. "You've got to come home right now," she'd told Dad on the phone. "Your son is driving me crazy." Having to leave the office for *that* unsettled his mind. When he blew in the front door he was one word away from coming for me.

"Dad," I said quickly, "She won't let me go out. She thinks you get colds from the cold because it's the same word."

He wasn't interested. "All right, Millie, what happened?"

"He called his mother a bitch."

That was the word. Dad charged me with a kick in the thigh and a fist on the shoulder while Mother had his arm shouting, "Robert! Robert!" Later, when he was becalmed, he sat next to me, silently at first.

"You got to go down and tell your mother you're sorry," he told me. "I can't be called home from the office to settle things. Please. For me."

"I made kibbee nayee for you, just the way you like it," Mother said, and went to the refrigerator.

I had tried to make sense of her food preparation. Her cooking times were calculated by how long it takes to kill suspected organisms. Her pot roasts emerged from the oven desiccated. Her peas in the pot were a lumpy light green paint. She must have learned at the School of Cordon Sanitaire. But kibbee nayee is raw lamb or beef with bulgar wheat. RAW! If that same meat went into making a hamburger it would have been cooked to death. A rose by any other name was anything but.

We sat in the breakfast room with Syrian bread and the platter of kibbee that was drowning in olive oil. Was there some attribute that olive oil hadn't been credited with? I watched Mother spoon out a chunk as the oil rushed in to fill the hole. When Dad called to say he'd be late I told her I couldn't wait, and left.

In my next session with Dr. Kimbrough I recounted the terror of seeing my father lose control. "Dad never sided with me," I told Dr. Kimbrough. "Never. He always sided with Mother."

"So, if you can't beat 'em, join 'em," he said.

I didn't understand and he asked, "Who would a son want to identify with, a weak father or a strong mother?"

"Dad weak?!"

"He didn't stand up to your mother. And when *you* did, that was threatening to him and he had to crush your rebellion. Father is pretty scary when he lost control but Mother could control him. She could turn him on and turn him off. Not a bad power to have."

I nodded. And wondered: if I didn't identify with Dad, what would that make me? ...

VI

… A playboy. Not the ass man in Playboy Magazine. Somebody mollycoddled who didn't want to work, Grandfather would say. Somebody who'd marry for money and be supported, Dad would add. He'd be what that purple fop in Grandfather's painting would grow up to be, I'd have said. But we'd all agree: there was no one more despicable.

At age 25 I could have passed for one. Christiane was pretty and she was teaching me French. Sally and I lazed on the bed smoking while the stereo played Horace Silver and John Coltrane. I watched Doris paint and tried to understand abstract expressionism. Just look and feel, she said, but I suspected her of trying to give it a mystique. There was still the occasional all night poker game at Phi Delta Phi and afternoons at the Michigan Union playing three cushion billiards. In one game I was averaging two billiards every three turns, twice my average, and against Fat Carl who had the best stroke. But when I realized I was beating him my game fell off and he won. I didn't need Dr. Kimbrough to tell me why, but hearing it—it stung.

"You took aim at the king, and you had him. But—you let him off. You got scared. 'Really, Mr. Carl, I'm not challenging you. See how poorly I'm playing? I'm not a threat.' "

That was me, alright, getting into fights as a kid and if I was winning, giving up. My perfect losing record had Dad puzzled. He and Grandfather both had welcomed fights, and once, together, knocked some men around in a billiard hall and threw them out. So, Dad hired the neighborhood tough,

Playboy, Northwestern University, 1956

Don Korth, to box with me in our basement. Why would Dad pay *him*, I wondered. Korth was happy to box me for free. *I* was the one that needed to be paid. A year later, when I was thirteen, I shot a paper wad at a dwarf on a motor scooter, who promptly got off and knocked me down. Poor Dad, when I had to tell him that his son had been felled by a bad-ass dwarf. He needed a geneticist to reassure him that genetics is a tricky business and that, as an unsuccessful sire, he was in good company with some famous racehorses and champion field trial dogs.

I did change, physically, after my plebe year at military school when I asked to play varsity football. "Gain fifty pounds," Coach Oliver replied, dismissively. "We need a defensive tackle." That was what Dad had been waiting for. "This summer you'll be unloading boxcars at the warehouse," he told me. "For lunch it'll be steak and eggnog. After work go lift weights at the Y." I had left Culver weighing 147. I returned weighing 200. And I played, and even scored a touchdown. Dad thought football had remade me. But billiards said otherwise.

I graduated from the law school and passed the bar exam. That was the end of the line. Last stop: Hamady Bros. I would now have to confront my father.

"I'm sorry, Dad. I'm really sorry."

"You're sorry!" he said, measuring his next words. "Your life has been soft … and you are soft … and *I* am sorry. But it's all right. It's all right. You're the eldest so naturally I was looking to you. But I don't need you. Your brother is doing a good job. He's married and settled down. He has a lovely wife. You don't like the business? Fine. You'd just gum up the works. All right, you've made your choice. You want to go your own way. Go ahead. And no hard feelings. Honestly. Goodbye and good luck."

Those last four words: wasn't this Grandfather and his son Louie redux?

That evening Dad called. "Let's keep things the way they are. You'll keep coming up Wednesday afternoons to pay for your psychiatric and you'll see your mother. And who knows what's in the future."

Finally, no more subterfuge ... not with Dad, anyway. I had a profession in mind when I flew to Washington, D.C. My interview with the C.I.A. took place at a folding table in an abandoned building downtown. I was smiling as I sat. "So, what are you interested in," the interviewer asked. "Cloak and dagger," I replied. He delved into my Middle East background and invited me out to Langley for two more interviews. "We'll get back to you," I was told.

Four months passed. I gave up hearing from the C.I.A. and enrolled in graduate philosophy at the university. Then a letter arrived from Langley. "We have what we think you're looking for," was all it said. I was intrigued. An invitation to become our man in Aleppo? No, it had come too late. I was more interested now in why you can't step in the same river twice.

That fall of 1962 I moved in with Doris. She was tall with auburn hair and her studio was chockablock with paintings and stretched canvases and twisted oil paint tubes lying about. There were two floor-to-ceiling cages, one for a spider monkey and his capuchin cousin, the other for finches. She was indifferent to their shit which often landed outside the cage. In their reaction to shit Doris and Mother would bracket everyone else on Earth.

"Are you sure you want to be hooked up with an artist?" Dr. Kimbrough asked me. "She's free form and you like structure. She creates with medium and you with ideas. How compatible are you?"

He sounded disturbingly like Dad.

"I ask only two things from you," Ted and I heard early on from Dad. "You get in the business. And you marry your own kind."

But he wasn't asking. He was telling.

Cousin Evelyn did not marry her own kind. She ran off with an American soldier in 1944. Dad told us, Ted and me, that she was a bad girl who had done a bad thing and if she approached us, from then on, we were to turn and walk away. "You are Druze because both your parents are Druze," Dad said, "in a chain that goes back a thousand years. There is no conversion. Once that chain is broken, its broken for good."

Years later we learned that her older brother, who was born in the old country—(Evelyn was born here and was a bobby soxer)—rose up at a family gathering and proclaimed that whoever invites his sister to their home will never again have him as their guest. And Dad *amened* it. Evelyn was out of the family. She became a sad figure wandering the periphery after her divorce.

RULE. THIS BEING AMERICA, YOU ARE FREE TO MARRY THE DRUZE OF YOUR CHOICE.

Dad was a zealot. His immortality was at stake. But he wasn't a prude.

"If you're in a gangbang, and she gets pregnant," he told us when we were teenagers, "with the Hamady name on supermarkets all over town and your father and grandfather regularly in the news, she'll finger you for the father. If that happens, I'll make your life hell."

RULE. IF SHE KNOWS WHO YOU ARE, YOU'RE NOT GETTING LAID.

In the summer, Cousin Karl and I would cruise Fenton Lake in our speedboat looking for girls, and sometimes we'd be successful. We passed ourselves off as Karl and Bob Hamilton up from Pontiac. Invariably, one of them would say,

"Aren't you one of the Hamady boys? My brother is a checker at your Third Avenue store."

Our cover would be blown. And there we'd be, dying of thirst on a poison pond.

Cousin Roy, who was in the war, gave us the American version of our rule. "You don't get your jam where you make your bread and butter." So where did *he* get his, we wondered: the Upper Peninsula?

Where *were* the Druze girls in America? They were at the annual Druze convention. The one Dad took us to when I was eighteen and Ted sixteen was at the Mayflower Hotel in Washington, D.C. There, inside the rookery, Dad selected one girl for serious consideration. "She's from an excellent family," he informed us.

RULE. THE MORE EXCELLENT IS THE FAMILY, THE LESS EXCELLENT IS SHE.

In this case I imagined her coming-out picture in the aptly named *Cleveland Plain Dealer*.

That evening Dad asked us, "Well, what do you think?"

"Come on, Dad," I said. "You're not serious."

"You want to know what I think of her?" he began with great solemnity. "Honest to God, I think she's a movie star."

Ted thought it was funny. Not I. I saw that he'd sacrifice me for his immortality. Just like he'd do for the business.

Until the early fifties, the Hamady family was a foreign culture living in Flint's midst, definitely a part of Flint and, as definitely, apart. Then Uncle Kay, followed by Dad, were invited to join the Flint Country Club. Aunt Hajar was exotic and sophisticated and Dad was running Hamady Bros. They accepted, and the two families became part of Flint's social rubric. But the club doors had closed to any more Hamadys, which fractured the family and began a process of dissolution and assimilation.

What remained unaffected and sacrosanct, however, was that Druze must marry Druze. So when Dad discovered I had a girlfriend at Northwestern University, at Christmastime he invited me into the living room for a formal discussion.

"Now, I want you to listen with an open mind," he began, pacing while I sat. "Suppose you had a dog. And let's say he's a collie. Would you tell someone you had an American dog? No. You'd say you have a collie. See? His kind is his breed. He has more in common with a collie in China than he does with the pointer next door. And you have more in common with a Druze, wherever she is."

"And *whoever* she is," I replied.

"Come on, this is serious," he warned. "You know you don't have to marry someone you don't like. You can marry any Druze you want."

"And keep the change," I replied.

He regarded me malevolently, then paced away pinching his lip. I reminded myself of his temper, but I felt flip.

"I tell you what," he said. "Since there's no getting through to you in the normal way we'll do a role reversal. I'll be you and you be me. But you got to really try. All right? I'll start. And now I'm you …

"I want to marry whoever I want, Dad, whether she's compatible with me or not. That's my right as an American. And if she's downstairs drinking cocktails while our children are upstairs crying and hungry, that's my right, too. Okay, Dad, what do you say to that?"

"Nope, you got to marry a Druze girl," I said.

He smiled. "Why, Dad? I'm all ears."

"Because she'll be compatible with your mother and me. And if you're made unhappy by that, that's unfortunate, but at least our grandchildren will be Druze."

He stared, motionless, while I imagined opposing forces clashing within. He looked like a wounded buffalo. Dangerous.

"Is that what you think?" he finally asked.

"That's what I think."

"All right. I admit that that's a factor. But I'm also thinking of your happiness."

"Come on, Dad!" I said. "Life, liberty, and the pursuit of happiness with a Druze wife. Is that what you taught us?"

"You're also, as my son, in charge of *my* happiness," he replied and shook his head. "And I cannot allow it to happen."

The following spring vacation I first visited my girl friend in Cincinnati. When I came home, as I was paying for the taxi, Dad walked down the drive. The taxi pulled away and I saw he had a .45 pistol in his hand.

"Come inside," he said.

I followed him up the drive. Mother's car was gone. Conveniently gone? I wondered. Was this drama really happening?

As soon as we were in the hall he turned and faced me.

"Are you going marry her?" he asked menacingly.

"Is that gun loaded?" I wondered aloud.

He set the .45 on the hall table and made a fist.

"Are you going to marry her?" he repeated in the same tone.

When I didn't answer he hit me hard in the chest.

"Are you going to marry her?"

I'd have been afraid to say yes and I was damned if I'd say no. He punched me again, hard.

"Are you going to marry her?"

My voice cracked when I said, "You're not going to get an answer like this."

"Then we'll go in the living room."

He took the gun and I followed him in. We sat 15 feet apart, facing one another. My hands were in my pockets so he couldn't see them trembling. The gun, I figured, was there to amplify his authority ... unless I confronted him, which I had no intention of doing. But this submission to a force majeure, this subjugation, was demeaning. Inside I burned with resentment. He had me now, but I wouldn't forget it.

"Now, are you going to marry her?" he asked, still in that matter-of-fact tone that said, "Because if you are ..."

... what? What was he prepared to do?

"Is the gun loaded?" I asked.

"No," he answered, then his eyes flashed with anger. "Why don't you answer, God damn you?! Or are you already married?"

I let him think so, for a few seconds ... "No, I'm not married. It's not that serious. But it's not your business."

He leaned back in this chair. A long silence followed while he stared down at his feet. His head was nodding when finally he looked up.

"You want to go to law school," he said, slowly. "I'll have to sell that to your grandfather. And you'll expect me to pay for it, of course. And give you an allowance. So, I'll make you a deal. Next summer you'll make a trip back to the old country. And Aunt Selma will take you around, you and your brother, to meet some Druze girls. And you'll give marriage an honest-to-God chance. Then, at the end of the summer, if you've really tried and nothing has come of it, I'll support you through law school …

"*And* I'll get off your back about marrying a Druze girl."

There it was. He had lost. When I nodded he came over and held out his arms. I stood and it was a different man that I embraced. Gone was the hero who came home from work and invited Ted and me to "jump on and tell me when you're on," then suspended us overhead in each hand.

This man was limited …

a desperate man …

mortal.

VII

In the summer of 1959 Mother's sister in the old country was commissioned to select Druze girls for Ted and me to visit. Younger than Mother, and sweeter, Aunt Selma had the same expressive eyes and soft form. Ted arrived early with Mother and was waiting while I enjoyed a brief vacation in Europe with some law school friends. We bought motorcycles in Cologne and biked down to Pamplona to run with the bulls. I left some flesh on the road south of Orleans when my bike upturned on gravel. In the Pamplona corrida a crowd of runners parted suddenly for a bull steaming toward me that knocked me flat. Then in Madrid I hooked up with a beautiful woman for a four day affair. I arrived in Beirut scraped up, broke and with the clap. Two days later we were off for the first visit.

When the limousine pulled away from Mother's village of Ras el Metn—Ted, Mother and I in the back seat, Aunt Selma and Uncle Amin in front with their chauffeur, Joseph—I knew nothing, not where we were going, who we were seeing or whether there were any important rules of address and comportment. Ted was content to sit back trusting and see what comes. Not I. This was a time for vigilance. But for what? Were people going to observe the girl and me, tally up where we appeared to fit and didn't fit and compare score cards? Where was the neutral zone between being too aloof and too friendly ... between being seen as discourteous and being regarded as now engaged? In my state of mind no scenario was too wild to be imagined.

Ted, Mother and me with Aunt Selma and Uncle Amin, Bhamdoun, 1959

"Bob, this is Lena. Lena, this is Bob. Bob, do you take this girl…."

We had passed one village and were coming up to the town of Hummana but no one had talked. The atmosphere in the car was solemn, purposeful: the Burghers of Calais in a Cadillac.

"Her name is Layla," my aunt finally volunteered, "and she is young, very smart in school, a lovely girl, already she has several suitors. After you meet her I think we can throw away the list."

Had my aunt seen her? No. But the information came from a very good source. Who?

"Somebody who knows her well," Mother said, brusquely. "You don't know them."

The picture that was forming in my mind was of a girl veiled but not for religious reasons.

"Will somebody please tell me what happens when we get there?" I begged.

"Aunt Selma worked hard to arrange this," Mother said. "You leave it to her. All you have to do is be a gentleman, smile, don't start mouthing off, and just leave the *rest* to her."

"Yes, but what *is* the rest?"

"Don't sweat it, Bob," Ted said from the other side of Mother. "They're not going to marry you against your will."

"It's easy for you to be nonchalant."

"You may be the oldest," Mother said, "but they want to meet your brother, too. You're not the only God's gift to women."

"Don't be asinine," I told her.

"Mister Bob is going to meet Layla," Joseph sang into the mirror. "Mister Bob, this is our Layla. Isn't she a lulu?"

Aunt Selma laughed and told Joseph in Arabic to keep his eyes on the road. Joseph was not the kind of scary chauffeur who drove in the passing lane while muttering, "*They'll* yield." But I'd already seen him hit an elderly woman on a crowded street in Beirut, sending her up in a somersault. "Watch where you're going," he yelled and gestured out the window as she landed.

"Hey, Ted, I wonder what they've been told about us?" I asked him.

"I told them that you are very handsome and very well educated. . . ." Aunt Selma answered before Mother interrupted.

"Aunt Selma has to exaggerate. People expect it. If she describes you as you really are they would think *that* was an exaggeration and that maybe you looked like phantoms of the opera. Aunt Selma told them the right thing. Just leave it to her."

Uncle Amin who had said nothing now began whistling the wedding march. A big man with a low hairline, he looked like a Mexican bandit from a silent film. He'd emigrated to Venezuela and made millions with appliance distributorships, after a decade of playing poker and drinking vodka. He was my favorite uncle.

Joseph stopped the car alongside a tall stucco wall that guarded the privacy of the villa inside. As we emerged from the car into the quiet cool of late afternoon no one appeared to greet us. We were more than an hour late and the thought that the host had vacated was tantalizing. I lagged behind with Joseph as the others made for the gate.

"Maybe they got tired of waiting and went off," I said to Joseph.

"No, Mister Bob. They're inside still getting ready. This is Lebanese time. If we had fought with the allies in the war we would just now be landing in Normandy."

"*Ehlan*" and other welcoming noises erupted from inside. Joseph arched his eyebrows and, smiling, twisted the ends of his imaginary mustache. I entered the gate and passed under the shade of a lovely loquat tree to join the line of our entourage walking around shaking hands, done in the Lebanese manner of lifting a limp hand and smiling without introduction. Among the aunts and uncles and cousins in the receiving line, I counted three possible Laylas. The real one was identified as soon as I stepped inside.

"Please, why don't you sit here next to Layla."

The man I presumed was her father, small, bald, in a sport jacket and sandals, led me out of the drawing room into an adjoining alcove and gestured at the divan. I sat staring straight ahead as she sat down beside me. Everyone was sitting side by side around the drawing room laid out like a doctor's waiting room. Layla's father leaned towards Mother, listening as she gabbed. No one looked at us, as if to confer privacy while we *got down to business*. A maid entered the alcove with a tray of demitasse. I passed it up and so did Layla. I hadn't really seen her, and I wasn't going to look now.

I thought of the friends I'd been biking with in Spain, cruising now to Marseilles and the Riviera. If they could have seen me sitting there, plucked and oven ready. "Come on, Hamady," I imagined them saying, "you gotta find out if she's a virgin." That much they knew about.

RULE. NO CHERRY, NO MARRY.

Virgins! The Arabs could have them in *their* paradise, those blissful girls in stiff dresses I went out with when I was sixteen who answered my advances with, "Please don't spoil the evening."

Dante had the appropriate hereafter for virgins.

"ABANDON HOPE ALL YE WHO ENTER"

Layla's presence was growing. The pressure to say *something* was building. I was insulting her by not speaking, wasn't I? Maybe she hated this, too. Maybe she had a boyfriend in college but she was told you got to meet this guy whose grandfather owns a large enterprise in America by a great lake. No one was looking … still not looking. …

"Um … Do you go to American University of Beirut?"

"I have another year to take my baccalaureate."

She was small with brown hair. Pretty eyes, I supposed. Spoke good English.

"Baccalaureate?" I wondered aloud. "And then you graduate from the University?"

"Then I shall go to the university."

So, she was 17, maybe even 16. And she had suitors? Probably some randy old Arabs stroking their beards while examining the goods.

"And you are at the University of Michigan?" she asked.

"Yes, in the law school."

"And after, you will go to be in the …"

She paused, but I had ceased to listen. Something had changed. The conversation had stopped! Mother, Layla's father, everyone, they were looking this way with smiles of benediction! I tensed.

"*Baba, comment se dire la societé famille?*" I heard Layla ask.

"I think she asks if you will enter into your family enterprise," her father said to me.

"Oh, yes," Mother answered. "Bobby is going to follow in his father's footsteps. He has two more years. Teddy, too. He has …"

"Excuse me," I interrupted, rising from the divan. "I'm going to see that beautiful tree out there."

"Of course," said Layla's father. "Layla will show it to you."

I wandered out, followed by Layla. At the loquat tree she said, "It is beautiful yes, and very old. In Arabic we say *akadinny*. Do you speak Arabic?"

I dropped my hands into my pockets and turned. "It must be hard having to meet men like this with everybody looking."

"It is our way," she said. Then, smiling, "I think it is not your way."

We talked easily, knowing nothing would come of it. The visit ended and on the ride back Aunt Selma dismissed the experience as a first visit and was touting the next girl on the list. But now I knew what was coming. We would be taken on three more visits to meet four girls, two in one family. Then it was over. For me. Ted had fallen in love with a Druze girl whose father was the Saudi Ambassador to the United States, and got engaged. Dad wrote,

"For me to say I am the happiest man in Flint would be putting it mildly."

Now with his Druze immortality seemingly assured for another generation, Dad threw up his hands as they might do in Al Anon and let go of my life. When I informed him in early 1964 that Doris and I were getting married, I could almost hear him shrug on the phone.

With Mother, marrying a Druze was never an emotional issue for reasons I never understood. That didn't mean she was without comment when I told her . . .

"Ah, Bobby, anything to be different. I thank God we didn't have two of you. Well, I hope she makes you happy, Son."

The following May we were married in a quiet ceremony at the Unitarian Church. There was Dad, past president of Flint Chamber of Commerce and an old Roosevelt hater with his arm around Doris' father, who ran for mayor of Jersey City on the Socialist ticket. Mother was gracious to the bride while informing her that, "You know, Bobby could have had one of the Ford (Henry Ford) girls."

We honeymooned in the Caribbean and returned to painting and philosophy. But as autumn progressed so did a new syndrome. Studying now felt like an enema buildup. I began every Monday morning empty and by Wednesday afternoon I was bloated and wanting to blast out of the library. In November, I dropped my courses and went hunting. When I started up again in February so did the pressure.

"I need answers," I demanded from Dr. Kimbrough.

"I want what I want when I want it," he answered.

That was Kimbrough's way of saying I was being infantile. Any criticism of him now would be more baby talk. How was it that I could be infantile but he couldn't be a quack? In April I dropped my courses again and passed up the preliminary exam.

In June Doris and I flew to Europe to look at art and do some serious eating. From Italy we flew to Greece, then to Lebanon where Aunt Selma and her brother awaited us. Doris was affectionately welcomed, but in an aside as we walked to the limousine, my uncle, who I thought resembled the composer, Prokofiev, said he wished I had married a Druze. My aunt in her aside informed me that *we* were not speaking to Cousin Najeeb nor to Cousin Arif. For how long? For however long.

RULE. A FEUD ENDS WHEN ONE DISPUTANT VISITS THE DEATHBED OF THE OTHER, BUT RESUMES IF THERE IS A RECOVERY.

We stayed with Aunt Selma in their swank Beirut apartment. What a difference was Beirut now from when I was here at age 11. That Lebanon of 1947, slow, Biblical and seemingly timeless had become the most recent stratum of buried civilization underneath the high-rise apartments, office buildings and widened roads heavy with the traffic of Cadillacs and Mercedes. I had never before seen crowds of beggars, mostly children wanting to sell us Chicklets gum. They were gone now, as were the hawkers bent over from the merchandise on their backs, and the donkey riders in the streets.

I found a pickup basketball game by the university outside at midday when the pavement blistered. Doris shopped and bought a Roman stone capitol—from Palmyra, the merchant assured her. She asked my aunt if the museum would certify it. Of course, she said, for whatever Doris wished it certified as. How about Aztec?

In the vendors shops I was seen as a generic American. But when over Arabic coffee they discovered my background, then they had to find out *who I was* ...

"Where are you from, you're American? ...

"Yes, of course I know Detroit. What is your background, Italian or French? *Paisan*, I think ...

"Your parents are Lebanese? From what village? ...

"So, they're Druze. And their names? ..."

It was all too familiar.

RULE. YOU WILL KNOW FRIEND OR FOE BY HIS FAMILY.

Him: "My great grandfather was your mother's great aunt's brother-in-law."

You: (Embrace and kiss him) "Cousin!"

Him: "Your sister-in-law's sister is married to my mother's sister's brother-in-law."

You: (Embrace and kiss him) "Uncle!"

Him: "No, my mother's family did not support Sheik Al Atrash against the French in 1925."

You: (Spit to the side, thinking) Scum!

We rented a car and drove up into the hills to Dad's village of Baakleen, as I'd promised him. The route now was new, straight, very different from the series of switchbacks that was the only way up in 1947. Dad was leaning on the horn for ten minutes as we made that climb, and he kept honking as our car wound through the narrow street hemmed in by ancient stone dwellings and shops. The crowd was waiting by Grandmother's house and quickly enveloped the car. When Ted and I finally made it into Grandmother's house Dad was waiting, standing behind her chair, his hand on the shoulder of an old woman with her veil drawn back, smiling broadly.

"Boys, this is my mother," he said, wiping his eyes.

We bent down to be embraced.

At bedtime Mother put vaseline on our cheeks that had been rubbed red by bristled beards and mustaches. We moved our bowels in Grandmother's gravity toilet, shooed the chickens off the window sill and went to sleep under mosquito nets.

Baakleen now was still much as it was then: insular and traditional. Doris was excited. What were people like who weren't gaga about animals?

In the village we were warmly greeted by two of Grandfather's nephews wearing the white turbans of holy men. Doris remarked on their blue eyes. They understood and smiled, stroking their beards, and in their expression I saw Grandfather's look of amusement.

Off to Lebanon, 1947

Dad, me and aunts, Baalbec, 1947

We had not progressed far from our car when other villagers approached, some shy, standing back to observe, some with photographs of Dad and Grandfather taken there or sent from Flint. Mother told us even Grandfather forgot how to write in just Arabic—he didn't get past the sixth grade—so his letters back to Baakleen were sprinkled with English words written in Arabic and Arabic words written in English. And since any word from an important man may be important, his letters were read aloud in the village council and the words pronounced and mulled over to decipher them.

Several of the villagers had stories of Grandfather coming to America. I was interested to hear and a translator was selected.

"Mahmud, he working on house, he stone mason," the translator began from the several accounts coming at the same time. "Somebody, his sister maybe, he hear her, she talk about money come to her from America, and Mahmud he drop his tools and say to his father, Hassan.... No, he not tell his father ... he tell him he want to work in Unteh, a Druze village, he not say he want go to America. His father he find out and he send Slayman, he brother to Mahmud, to go with gold to Beirut to bring back Mahmud. Slayman see him at port with gold. But Mahmud he not come back."

"Sooo," I said to the translator, "My grandfather disobeyed his father and lied to him."

That was translated back into Arabic, to everyone's great amusement.

Bou Nadim, who became Dad's surrogate father when Grandfather emigrated, remembered my reciting my full Arabic name when we were there in 1947 and asked me to recite it again. *"Hassan, shoo ismoo bil Araby?"*

"Hassan, Selem, Mahmud, Hassan, Mohammed, Alamedin, Hassan Hamady."

They were all smiling now, not from delight I thought but from satisfaction. *Tamaam!* Exactly!—was what their smiles communicated, as if, at that moment, my American look and manner and talk and wife were only vestments clothing a kinsman. Your kind is your breed, Dad said. I might have extended my arms and, by saying, *Kam baroodi*—How many guns?—received their aid. But I would never have asked because I wouldn't have been prepared to give it, not on the sole basis of kinship. I was not bound. I had to be free to choose. Whatever my breed, and I felt a bond with Bou Nadim and Baakleen, my heart was with Thomas Jefferson . . .

. . . as perhaps was Grandfather's heart. Hadn't he chosen freedom over loyalty to *his* father? I found myself smiling inwardly at this shared character with HIM, of all people!

Dad's mother had remarried after Grandfather divorced her, and Dad's half brother, Khalil, came now from the fields to welcome us. He spoke with a nervous laughter that caused Doris to regard me with arched eyebrows. When one of Grandfather's nephews invited us to dinner, Khalil firmly reminded him that, as the closer relation, *he* would be our host. In his rebuke, I saw that we should first have gone to seek him out. And I didn't inquire about those close to him as he now inquired about each member of my family. . . . "How is your dear father, and your mother? . . . And your brother, how is he? . . . And your grandfather, I hope he is well. . ."

RULE. WHEN INQUIRING INTO THE WELLBEING OF ANOTHER'S FAMILY, BEGIN WITH THOSE CLOSEST AND CONTINUE UNTIL THE RESPONSE IS, "WHO IS SHE?"

Uncle Jim, who never forgot a birthday or memorial day, called once and began his inquiries shouting above a fire alarm ringing in the background. Only when he had come to the end did he cry out, "Please, come turn this thing off, it's driving me mad."

But then,

RULE. EVERY INQUIRY INTO YOUR FAMILY MUST BE CANCELLED OUT BY A RECIPROCATING INQUIRY OR BY GIVING THEIR REGARDS.

"Hello, Cousin. How's everybody with you?"

"They're fine. They all say hello. How's the baby?"

"Baby's fine. He'd want to be remembered. By the way, I was sorry to hear about your uncle drowning."

"Thank you. I'm sure his last thoughts were with your family."

Two days later I drove with Doris to Ras el Metn, and what a difference was Mother's house and upbringing from the simple stone huts and terraced plantings of Dad's village. On his return from Brazil Grandfather Abbas had built a tall house with a courtyard on spacious grounds just down the hill from the one village street, with views into the valley cultivated with peas, beans and corn, and across to the villages of Brummana and Beit Mery perched on the next ridge. His poor relatives were employed in some capacity in the kitchen or bedrooms or on the grounds; and poorer ones, the ones who came to the front entrance with empty gunny sacks, were sent around to the stockhouse by the kitchen to fill their sacks with flour, oil, dried peas and maybe honey and pine nuts. Because of his largesse and local standing as the Druze *zaeem* (leader)of Ras el Metn, Abbas Salha could have fielded an armed company of Druze men and women to meet an outside threat.

Mother said that her feet did not touch the ground—she was carried everywhere by her aunts and fed the sweetest morsels from the lamb—until she was two. Her father, she said, was one of the Druze the French sought to cultivate in their efforts to administer their Syrian protectorate, and French generals and officers of high rank came to sit with him in his parlor, sharing Turkish coffee and French cigarettes while discussing solutions to some particular problem with the rebellious Druze. And, she said, she had sat on the lap of General Gamelin and knew Captain or Major deGaulle. About *that* I wondered. She'd also said she was born in 1916 when it was in fact 1912 and that she'd studied political science at the Sorbonne though she hadn't. She reminded me of the Lebanese merchant who sold Cousin Bobby Sol a blue white diamond and, when he was found out, said, "Blue-white, yes, but I didn't say blue-white-white." DeGaulle, yes, but did she say Charles?

When we were here in 1947 we mostly stayed in Ras el Metn with Mother's family. The house had one critical feature: flush toilets. Dad and Mother were daily occupied socially here and elsewhere. Ted and I went to a theater in Hammana and saw *Santa Fe Trail*. Otherwise, nothing changed from day to day. I was soon bored, and finding fault with everything: the smells of cumin from the kitchen, orange blossom in the lemonade, and urine off the hot pavement. There was too much dust, too many yellow jackets around the hanging Lebanese ice cream, the same white stone everywhere. I chased the neighbor's sheep away from their grazing and threw stones at their chickens, putting them to flight. I told the villagers of the wonderful life across the sea: the straight streets and green lawns and sitting at the soda counter at Le Mieux drug store with the latest Plastic Man comic sipping a lime phosphate.

One day in August I awoke with terrible stomach cramps. Malaria was the diagnosis of the village doctor. Three days after my appendix ruptured he changed his diagnosis. I bequeathed the bubble gum and baseball cards kept under my pillow to Ted and was rushed to Beirut to be operated on. When I came to, there was a plastic tube inserted in the hole on my right side that dripped poison into a basin. Mother was sitting on the bed. "Last night in Ras el Metn everyone in the village lit candles," she told me, "and they went in a procession to the grave of my father and prayed that you'd come through."

Doris and I returned to Ann Arbor. The war in Vietnam was escalating, and Dad wondered where I stood.

"Johnson is railroading us into an immoral war," I answered.

"You're an American," he said. "The enemy of America should be your enemy."

Nothing had changed between us.

"Sometimes, my son, you gotta fight," he said, nodding.

"This ain't the right time," I said but he went on nodding. Is there ever a right time for you? his expression asked. I ignored it.

Then, in December, I terminated psychotherapy. Four years was enough. But when the last session arrived, I wavered. Invisible tears were falling. Maybe this is premature, I said. How do I know if I'm cured?

Dr. Kimbrough laughed. "Let's just say this: you came because you didn't know who you were. If you know who you are ... *and* you accept it. How's that?"

"But I still don't know," I protested.

"When you do, you'll let me know," he replied and stood.

I raised myself off the couch and we shook hands. Then we parted.

Outside, in the light, I smiled. I was out of the repair shop. I'd broken out of my father's orbit. I'd married how and whom I wanted and the business no longer beckoned like a dead Ahab on Moby Dick.

I never had it so good.

VIII

"*B*obby, promise me ..." Dad began again in his monotone. He lay slightly elevated on the hospital bed with his face turned to me. His hand was limp in mine.

"*... you'll get in the business.*"

"I promise, Dad."

He smiled and his head turned away. The smile remained after his eyelids dropped, then faded with the deep breathing.

"He's asleep," Mother said and rose to cover him.

I presumed she regarded my promise to Dad for what it was: a simple courtesy to a dying man.

The following day when I visited him with Ted, he was unable to count past five. He asked us to harmonize a few old songs that he liked, then fell into sleep. Two days later he was comatose. He regained consciousness briefly when the tumor outran its blood supply, then lapsed back and the door closed behind. He was brain dead and put on life support.

What a predicament. Only three months before he was stricken Dad had purchased 14 stores from National Tea Co. which was going out of business. Hamady Bros. had just grown from 22 stores in Genesee County to 36 stores throughout Eastern Michigan.

"It's expand or die!" he'd declared dramatically on the phone.

I'd been surprised enough to call Mother.

"He didn't tell anyone, not even Jack," she said. "I don't know what possessed him. He should be cutting back. He's going to be 58 next month. Instead he goes out and buys four-teen stores."

"Cutting back would probably kill him," I said. "He's doing what he loves."

"What about me," she answered. "Don't I count for something? You know, Bobby, in Lebanon, men when they have money, they have leisure, they relax, they enjoy conversation, their family, they travel, they read. When I married your father that's what I thought, not go-go-go all the time. Every evening I'm with Hajar and Lily because our husbands are always working. How long have I been waiting so your father and I can take a trip around the world, go see the pyramids? And now he goes and buys fourteen more stores. It's selfish."

When I hung up I was picturing her in 1935, about to experience what her life would be like in America. Grandfather was waiting on shore as their ship, S.S. Manhattan, docked in New York. "Now, if you want to please *me*," Dad said, taking her arm, "please my father."

"And I did try," Mother told me. "Robert and his father had been living together in a suite of rooms at the Durant Hotel and now Dad—I have to start calling him Dad—as soon as we're on shore he hands us the keys to a house he'd bought for the three of us. I'd married a *pair* of men. And your grandfather was a wild man. He'd call from the City Club to say he was bringing four of his cronies over for dinner and would I make three chickens stuffed with Arabic rice. I didn't know how to cook, my aunts did all the cooking. I had to learn. Then when he arrived he'd want to show off his grandson. I'd say, 'Please, Dad, he's sleeping,' and he'd say he wouldn't wake you up but he always did and he'd parade you around and it would take me an hour to get you calmed down and

"I married a pair of men," Mother said

Grandfather and me, 1936

back to sleep, you'd be crying so hard. Then when he went back to the old country and got remarried I thought we could have our life back, but then Saada died in childbirth and we moved back in with him. And when your father went into the State Troops your grandfather would have his lady friends over to play cards and I'd have to sit there with them the whole time in case one of the women wanted to claim that he had said or done something. And I put up with it all these years. I put up with that insufferable man. And I did it to please my husband."

I could have told her Dad could live another thirty years and he'd still have her waiting. Hell, he wasn't interested in the pharaohs' tombs. Only in his own: the business.

But what was Hamady Bros. without Dad *alive*? I decided to see for myself. I hadn't been in the company's office since Dad's expansion. Now I found myself driving there with a foreboding.

I pulled into the president's parking space, went upstairs into the reception area and walked down the long hall to Dad's office. Into that chamber had streamed buyers, supervisors, merchandisers, layout people, foremen, salesmen with special promotions, emissaries—bringing information, awaiting instructions, carrying them out. Here was where everyone congregated on Grandfather's birthday and, with the meat manager leading, sang into the speakerphone:

"How do you do, Uncle Mike, how do you do,
"How do you do, Uncle Mike, how are you.
"We are with you to a man,
"We'll do everything we can,
"How do you do, Uncle Mike, how do you do."
That office was now dark.

Across the hall Ted's office was empty. I stood there, listening. A group of clericals were conversing in the next room. Somebody was leaving to go back into the General Motors shops. Somebody was staying until the company was sold. There was a rumor that K-Mart was buying it. A store manager was talking with K-Mart. Robert's dead, somebody said, but the family was hiding the news. "What are *you* going to do?" someone asked.

I walked to the clerical department and looked in.

"How's your father?" someone in the group asked.

"He's in a coma."

They were silent, and remained silent as I looked around the room. The number of clericals had doubled since the expansion. Some were sitting looking out. Others glanced up regularly. Where was the supervision?

I walked back down the hall where the buyers were bantering easily with the salesmen as if they were on their break.

Down the stairs and out into the warehouse dense with pallet upon pallet of cartons of food piled high and into the aisles, I followed a labyrinthine route to the loading dock.

"Jesus, Bill!" I began before he interrupted.

"There's not a God-damned thing I can do about it. Since we purchased them fourteen stores we got no space. Got to move goods to get at other goods. Payrolls doubled. Nobody knows what we got. Can't trust the stock status reports. Salesmen come down here and peer through the pallets and guess what there is. Nobody knows...."

"How's Robert?" he asked and I told him.

Slowly walking back to Ted's office I was wishing I hadn't come. Everywhere there was dysfunction and breakdown. Dad's expansion had the company severely stressed. Then he was struck down and everywhere there was apprehension. What was going to happen to the company ... to their jobs, their pay, their lives? Should they stay to find out? Other's were leaving.

In Ted's office, the CEO of Hamady Bros.' largest tenant turned as I entered.

"I was just telling your brother, your father promised to build a shopping center in Lapeer with a Yankee Store," he said. "He wrote it on the back of this."

In his open hand was a pack of matches with notes scratched inside.

"I told Joe if Dad agreed to it we'll do it," Ted said.

Joe appeared satisfied and nodded. "What's going to happen to the company now, if I might ask?"

"Nothing," Ted replied. "It'll go on just as before."

"Look, you know how close I am to your father," he continued. "So I want you to understand what I'm going to advise you now. You know we merged with Borman Foods out of Detroit."

Ted nodded.

"They've been doing what Hamady's should have started doing years ago. Their merchandising is as advanced as anything in the country. They know the movement of every item in every store every day. And they're aggressive. If they invade Flint with their Farmer Jack stores, which they probably will now that they have Yankee Stores, how could you compete? I don't think you'd stand a chance. Why don't you boys go down and talk with them. They might be interested in buying you out."

Joe strolled away leaving the two of us staring at each other. I asked Ted what he thought of Joe's speech.

"He's saying that to scare us into selling out for a song. He's Borman Foods now."

"You don't think there's any merit to what he says?" I asked. "This place is a mess."

"Look, Bob, I got work to do."

"Ted—," I began but his hands were up and his head was shaking.

I walked out and crossed into Dad's office, closed the door, and stood in the dark. The skin crawled on my arms and legs. Hamady Bros. vulnerability was frightening. And I was an outsider! Ted handled his anxiety differently. "Please, Bob, I don't want to hear," he was telling me, "I mustn't doubt." How did he do it? The evidence was everywhere.

I crossed back and looked in on Uncle Jack, Dad's cousin and cohort, a detail man, cautious and steady in contrast with Dad's wide-open flamboyant style of leadership. He looked up and waved me in. After we hugged he lamented, "You know, except for when Robert took you to Lebanon in 1947, he and I have never been apart. In Baakleen we all slept in the same bed with our mothers and Louie ... I can't believe it. I don't believe it...."

A short, wiry, intense man, a pious Druze who did not permit a wine sauce past his lips, he shook his head in disbelief. He attempted once to explain how we were related, saying that Dad was his mother's first cousin and his father's second cousin, then smiled at my bewilderment. Now, as the obvious successor to Dad, he did not inquire about the succession that probably Mother would determine. I probed into the health of the fourteen stores and he confessed that all but one were losing money and slipping in sales.

"But we're going to turn them around," he said, all enthusiasm. "How?"

"They're still run like National Tea Stores. We're going to put the old Hamady Bros. stamp on them."

The smile on my face was a false smile. They weren't going to turn those stores around, I felt, any more than they were going to turn Dad around. The management and management systems were obliterated. Pep talk and positive thinking wouldn't do it. Dad, the old country entrepreneur, had kept it a one man company, made it revolve around him after Grandfather, stitched himself into every function. Now, lying on his hospital bed, brain dead, the company he left behind still resembled the man, seemingly the same … from a distance.

And Mother? She claimed to have Grandfather's power of attorney, which would give her sole power. I decided to stop there on my way back to see what *she* was feeling, what she saw.

We sat in the living room with mint tea. The late afternoon light flooded in through the French doors, illuminating the reds and blues in the Kerman rug. The furniture was a mix of Mother's taste in French provincial, and some alabaster floor lamps and gilded mantleclock and bric-a-brac from the 1920's that came with the house. On the wall was a not very good painting of Lebanon's mountains and another oil of an Arabian casbah.

Mother's first words were that Dad would remain president for as long as he was alive. On life support that meant indefinitely. Sitting erect with her cup and saucer on a large floral sofa with her French porcelains and statuettes set about her she seemed informed of her power. Perhaps now, as the dowager baroness in her manor, she had found her rightful place in Flint.

"My father-in-law founded this company and my husband built it up," she said. "Now it's up to me."

On that, I laughed. "From grandfather to father to mother."

She stared back at me. My God, she was serious!

"Why not?" she asked, rhetorically. "Who says a woman can't run a company as well as a man? Joan Crawford is on the board of Coca Cola."

A movie actress is on the board of Coca Cola, so Mother, whose checkbook was balanced by Dad, can run the company. Again I laughed.

"Who else is there if not me?" she asked, then answered with mock incredulity. "You?"

"Mother, you don't know the first thing about running a company."

"And you do?" she answered and laughed. "You who's been a playboy all your life."

I had been laughing without realizing the rage building inside. From Grandfather to Father to Mother. As if I'd never been born. "What can *you* do?!" she was telling me and laughing. She could have added, "I ought to know. I raised you (to be that way): overdressed, overprotected, kept inside, enemas...."

And I was interpreting Mother's intentions as I had when I was five and about to have my tonsils removed. She had taken Ted and me to Dr. Stevenson's old mansion without explanation. Now, in his basement operating room she asked me to remove all of my clothes. I didn't trust her. If the surgery truly was on my throat I should be able to keep my underpants on. But Mother and the nurse stripped them off and put me in a robe, then held me down on the operating table while Dr. Stevenson applied the ether mask because I was screaming.

"Didn't you hear Dad make me promise to get in the company?" I heard myself asking.

"He wasn't himself," she replied. "If he wasn't ill, he would never have asked. Robert told me before he got sick, watch out for Bob, he'll be the Judas of the business. My husband, my dear Robert, he's counting on me, depending on me. I'm not going to let him down."

Without thinking I was on my feet and standing in front of Mother, above her really.

"You're not getting in that business," I told her. "You'll ruin it if you do, and you're not going to do it."

She attempted to rise but I pushed her back. She regarded me wide-eyed with alarm.

"If your father were here—,"

"He's not. And you're not getting into that company. If you try I'm going to stop you any way I can."

"You can't stop me!" she said triumphantly. "I've got the power of attorney."

"Try it, then. I'll get Ted and Uncle Jack and Uncle Kay. I'm going to stop you any way I can. It'll be a scandal."

She pushed on me to give her room. I retreated a few steps.

"What's gotten into you?" she wondered aloud. "Since when do you care about the company?"

Her question woke me up to myself in this ridiculous role. I retreated to my chair. My tone when I spoke was conciliatory.

"Look, Mother, I know you want to do whatever you can for the company. Because the company is really Dad. If the company lives, Dad lives. But the best thing you can do is stay in the background. For the company's sake. For Dad's sake."

She was quiet, pensive, nodding gently, her eyes fixed on me. She appeared to be accepting it. Had I done that? Something I needed to see Dad do and never did: stand up to Mother.

Driving back to Ann Arbor that evening, I tried to make sense of my feelings. I was ready to physically stop Mother from taking charge of a business I'd never given a damn about. Why? Was this something between Mother and me with the business incidental? Did the business represent Dad and I was protecting *him* from Mother? After four years of psychotherapy I was stranger to myself than I'd ever been.

The following day, Dr. Kimbrough had an afternoon cancellation and I went back.

"I don't know who I am. Heard that before?"

He was sitting like a mandarin with his hands folded in his lap, silently waiting. How to begin?

"My father is brain dead and the company is like an ant colony with the queen gone, utterly in chaos. I think my brother and Uncle Jack don't realize how serious it is. And to top it off, Mother who knows nothing about business and who emotionally...."

"I don't have to tell *you* about Mother!" I broke off, laughing.

"She wants to be chairman of the board," he said soberly.

I nodded.

"I feel sorry for you."

Of all the possible responses from Dr. Kimbrough—after all of his silences when I wanted answers, or "What comes to mind," or "You want what you want when you want it," or "Time's up"—now to hear that he felt *sorry* for me?!

"Can I ask *why* you feel sorry for me?" I asked.

"Your father's dying," he said. "And there's your grandfather's oracle. First and second generation of self-made men create a successful company and you and your brother—the silver spoon generation—will destroy it. If the business fails there won't be an asterisk after your names saying you inherited a failing business. The Flint newspaper will simply say that the company failed under you. And the oracle will come true."

"Wait a minute!" I said. "That's only if I get in the business. But I'm like Oedipus who finds out *before* he's married that this chick is his mother. Those problems were created by self-made men. And I'm not taking the rap."

I liked what I'd said. Bold talk. Because I was in the know. I saw what was coming. I could avoid the predicted outcome. I was in control of my fate. I wasn't a piece on the game board.

I went on to describe my confrontation with Mother. Dr. Kimbrough growled out a laugh.

"From Grandfather to Father to ... why, Mother, of course. But she's not getting in the business now. No way."

I was puzzled and asked what made him so sure.

"She's not going to play your role as the elder son because you showed her *you're* going to play it. You demonstrated, as between the two of you, who was the man. You *made* your decision about the business. You're in. You just haven't realized it yet."

Then, smirking at my bewilderment, "But *she* knows it."

When I found my voice, I protested. "But I don't want to get into the business."

"That's fine with Mother," he replied. "She's ready to play your role and give you her darning needles."

I was silent.

"What would they say if you didn't get in the business, I wonder?" Dr. Kimbrough began with mock contemplation. "Would they say that the eldest son fiddled in his ivory tower while the business burned?"

"Worse than that," I replied. "I promised Dad before he died that I'd join up. But I didn't consider it binding."

"Oh, that's even better," he said with undisguised relish. "They could say, 'Old Mike's eldest grandson had degrees in business and law and promised his father on the man's death-bed that he'd go into the company but when he saw the shape it was in he played it smart and ducked out. . . .

. . . Can you live with that?"

"I'd have to wouldn't I," I said with a shrug.

"No, you don't have to," he said. ". . . Don't you see that everything's changed? The man for whom you've held your-self back all your life—because you *love* him and don't want to displace him—*and* because you *fear* to displace him—is gone. This has released your aggression, as you demonstrated in stand-ing up to your mother. . . .

"Your father encouraged you to believe that his fate depended on you. And if you didn't tell your grandfather that you loved the business he'd sell out and hurt your father. And if you didn't submit to your mother she'd make his life miserable. With all that power, if you chose to assert yourself, *he'd* go down. You were in a zero-sum game with him. You loved your father and so you held yourself back."

"Oh, God!" I blurted out, covering my face, ". . . I know that in my soul . . . I know it. . . . That's how it is. . . . I love my Dad and I don't . . . don't want to hurt him. . . ."

I took some tissues and wiped my eyes.

"You weren't holding yourself back only out of altruism," he said. "With your power over his fate you were a threat. And you know how your father reacts to threats."

". . . I can feel that, too. . . ."

"Maybe you're better positioned now for what lies ahead," he said when I was composed. "Go home and talk about it with your wife. You have some catching up to do with your-self. . . .

"And good luck."

I left, shaking my head. That session had been like a trip through the funhouse at the old Flint Amusement Park, with scares in the dark, false doors and a sudden drop down a chute and out, where I find myself deposited at … where else?! Hamady Bros. I was going into the business.

At home, Doris was unhappy with my turnaround. I didn't think business, didn't dress business, didn't like it. I was betraying myself, and for what? For a family business I was sick to death of. I was letting this happen to me, letting them take away my resistance, my freedom, *"mon panache." She* was no longer sure who I was. She'd been married to an academic in a university town where the cinema showed Kurasawa, Bergman and Truffaut, and where the talk was Raushenberg and Diebenkorn, or Beat Poets like Ferlingetti, for whom the crucifixion meant, *They stretched the cat on a tree to cool.* Now she finds herself with a businessman headed for God knows what in Flint.

How could I tell her what happened when I wasn't sure myself?

It won't be for long, I said to her. And she didn't have to worry about moving. I didn't mind an hour commute if it wasn't stop and start. And did she see the irony of it all? There would be no welcome mats out for me. I was the last thing the company wanted.

"Nobody wants it but you're still going to do it," she said, shaking her head. "Do you really know what you're doing?"

No. Not even close.

IX

Next morning saw me driving our VW bug up to Flint. "First thing, buy yourself a nice Buick," I heard Dad tell me. If only he were conscious to see me then, motoring up to work in the grocery business. He'd have himself a good laugh; unless ... unless he had really confided to Mother that I'd be the Judas of the business. If he had, I wouldn't pretend to be surprised. The business was his child. I didn't love it. And now it was orphaned, and unprotected.

At the office I was greeted by a store supervisor who'd heard I was coming into the business. Dr. Kimbrough was right. Mother knew before I did. I asked him how *we* were doing with those fourteen new stores, but he wasn't ready to betray his feelings to an unknown.

"I always wondered about Jack and your dad," he said. "How them two are related."

"Dad is his mother's first cousin and his father's second cousin."

Then, noting his blank look, "That's what I say."

As I walked away I was laughing to myself wondering what the employees must think of all the old country stuff. When Hamady Bros. was unionized in 1961—which happened in the number one union town in America but was still a blow to the patriarchal Hamadys—Uncle Kay, Uncle Jack and Dad sat across the table from the Retail Clerks discussing their negotiating tactics openly and heatedly in Arabic, until finally the company lawyer declared in exasperation, "Are you going to let *me* know what we're doing?"

I was soon sitting with Uncle Jack and Ted at the conference table. The power vacuum left by Dad was palpable. Uncle Jack had been subordinate only to Dad, which meant, simply, that he was usually listened to. Now he was tentative, uncertain. Ted, reliant on Dad, looked closed down.

There was no position open, they said, so what did I have in mind? I proposed to research the company and write a report. They were happy to have me distant from the buying and selling of groceries. And I was content to come in as an internal consultant, an outsider with no title who might not be held responsible for the ship going down ... as the man who wasn't there.

Uncle Jack proposed that, while Dad was alive, the three of us run the company as a triumvirate. I was shocked at coming into that much power. That soon passed and I saw my opportunity for the one thing I knew.

"I think we're in real trouble with Dad's expansion," I declared. "It can't be absorbed and it'll bleed us to death. We got to sell those outlying stores and retrench to our primary marketing area and build a professional management."

Ted and Uncle Jack exchanged looks of surprise and found concurrence.

"We just bought those stores," Uncle Jack said. "If we buy them one day and sell them the next what would that do for morale? Ted, what's your opinion?"

"It would be a repudiation of Dad," Ted answered.

"I vote against it," said Uncle Jack. "Ted?"

"I do, too."

"Welcome to the business," said a smiling Uncle Jack.

Hmm. So that was the lineup. The *initial* lineup, I hoped, because if Dad's expansion was kept, I wasn't sticking around. Of the two, Uncle Jack was probably the more comfortable with the status quo. That made Ted the linchpin. But what could possibly induce him to change his mind? He sought stability. Uncle Jack *was* stability. In comparison with Uncle Jack, I'd just blown in from Borneo chanting and rolling the bones.

Mother said that Ted was a welcome change after me: unspoiled, undemanding and stable. I consoled myself that she favored those characteristics because he was from her side of the family. Which came through each time I called her.

"TEDDY?" ... "oh, hullo, bob"

I don't remember Dad ever raising a hand to Ted. He went to U. of M. as expected, majored in history, married well and correctly, then eased into the business as a grocery buyer and in four years was a vice president and director. "Your brother is doing commendably," Dad told me. Not mentioned was the Teaberry gum the salesman let Ted purchase in cartons instead of packages, a mistake that went unnoticed until another buyer called Ted's attention to the forty foot semi pulling up to the warehouse with a trailer banner proclaiming, "World's largest single order of Teaberry gum bound for Hamady Bros." It took Dad two years to give it away.

When the meeting broke up I followed Ted into his office and closed the door.

"Ted, we got to sell those outlying stores."

"How can you come flying in here and say we got to sell?!" he said, gesturing wildly. "Jesus, Bob! You haven't changed from when you were six and heard there was a priest in the house and you charged in yelling, 'Where's the priest?! Where's the priest?!'"

"Ted, unless those stores are sold we'll be bailing water on a sinking ship, and I'm not going down with it."

"You got to leave," he said, shaking his head.

"I can't do anything while we have those stores," I said. "You're the key."

"Don't put me in that position," he answered, pointing at me.

"One more thing, Ted, and then I'll leave. Consider this: if we keep those stores, what's the upside? We have an expanded company. The downside is that the company fails. That's what Grandfather is betting on. All other considerations mean nothing. THE COMPANY MUST NOT FAIL."

He nodded and asked me to go, but politely. As different as people said we were, we shared in what we had at stake here, which was more than what we did. It was who we were.

The following week we had the same talk. And the week after that. And the week after that, for two more months. He was exasperated. Fed up. Threatening even. I couldn't let up. I was certain. We had to jettison Dad's expansion. I'd give it until Christmas. If Ted hung on, I was getting off.

Then his daughter, Karen, was diagnosed with incurable cancer. For one week Ted and Saniya encamped with us in Ann Arbor while Karen underwent chemotherapy at the university hospital. Ted was benumbed. Dr. Kimbrough located a psychiatrist for him to talk to. The following Monday he returned to work. Shortly after,

"All right. I changed my mind."

"Are you sure?" I asked.

"I said so didn't I?"

I invited Uncle Jack into my office and broke the news. He turned solemnly to Ted.

"That's your dad's purchase, not mine, so don't think about me. Think how that will reflect on your father. Think of the effect on morale. Hamady Bros. has never retreated. Ted, you have to be absolutely sure."

Ted's lips were pursed. "I'm sure, Uncle Jack."

Uncle Jack was silent. "Then I'll make it unanimous," he said slowly. "We sell those outlying stores...

"Its God's will," he declared abstractly, as if he were trying to justify his vote to Dad. "Robert didn't buy those stores. The tumor made him do it."

Then, walking out with Ted, "Ted, I never thought you'd turn against me."

I poured myself an espresso and leaned back with my pipe. My office door like all the others was glass because Grandfather deemed privacy incompatible with selling groceries. A clerical paused to peer in as I was blowing smoke rings, then walked on with, I imagined, further evidence of the company's internal decay. She would have liked to know that Ted's change of vote, repudiating Dad, saved his company. Now we could move ahead.

We hired a property man from the Detroit division of Krogers to undo Dad's expansion and I took up the study of Hamady Bros. financial statements. I immediately saw that the company's profit peaked nine years ago in 1957, when Grandfather wanted to sell the business and Dad begged him out of it. During the next nine years Dad reinvested all of the profits into building more stores, over-saturating Flint. And profits declined. What was the goal?! I was turning my pen in my mouth, until I realized the answer was not in the numbers. Dad was ignoring return on investment to *protect* the grocery business from competitors. He was *mothering* the business.

Mother finally accepted that Dad wasn't coming back and he was taken off life support. It was January 12, 1966, and the funeral house was packed with family, employees, friends, grocery people, and the curious—650 people. Rising high above

—Journal Photo

RECEIVES MEDAL — Sheikh Michel al Khoury pins the Lebanon Order of Merit on Robert M. Hamady, president of Hamady Brothers, Inc. The medal, which is the highest honor the Lebanon government can bestow, was presented to Hamady for his contribution to better relations between the U.S. and Lebanon.

Hamady Given Highest Honor
Lebanese Government Offers

Robert M. Hamady, president of Hamady Brothers, Inc., Friday night was awarded the Order of Merit by the Lebanese Government for "his great American citizenship which has created a better relationship between the people of Lebanon and the United States."

The Order of Merit medal was given to Hamady at a dinner at the Flint Golf Club by Sheikh Michel al Khoury, president of the National Council of Tourists in Lebanon.

The medal is the highest honor that can be bestowed by Lebanon upon a private citizen, whether a citizen of Lebanon or of another country.

ACCEPTING the medal, Hamady told Sheikh al Khoury, "I regard it as one of the highest honors to receive an award for being a good American.

"To receive such an award from the country of my forefathers doubles my feeling of gratitude."

Hamady added that "being a good American is not only an obligation of all of us but it is a privilege as well."

He said, "Any contributions I have been able to make as an American can be made as well by any person who sincerely uses his best abilities in connection with the many opportunities that the United States extends equally to all."

Presenting the medal, Sheikh al Khoury said that it is a basic philosophy of the people and government of Lebanon that when its people migrate to other countries that they become good citizens of that country.

"Robert Hamady has more than adequately fulfilled that obligation," he said.

"BECAUSE HE has been such a good citizen of the United States he has brought great credit to the people of Lebanon and it is because of this that we present him with the highest honor possible of our government," Sheikh al Khoury said.

Sheikh al Khoury, who is the son of a former president of Lebanon, is among a group of foreign visitors who have been touring Michigan in a pre-Michigan Week visit.

Although the visit by the group has been plagued by inclement weather, Sheikh al Khoury did not appear to mind.

"The people I have met in Michigan have showed a warmth that no sun could match," he said.

VETERANS

VETERAN

ɡn Wars

MBER 12

All You Got

To Do Is

"SHOW GO" . .

Then Go Go Go!

R MAILE URGES

HE'S APPRECIATED: Robert H. Hamady (left), president and treasurer of Hamady Brothers, Inc., a chain of supermarkets with offices at 3301 South Dort Highway in Flint, is shown receiving an appreciation citation bearing the name of Andy Borg, the commander-in-chief of the Veterans of Foreign Wars of the U.S. from Cooper T. Holt, at the annual convention banquet held in the Grand Rapids Civic Auditorium. Holt is executive director of the VFW's Washington Office a n d was a former commander-in-chief. Hamady anonymously paid for a VFW staged party for 68 wounded Vietnam vets turned away from the Conrad Hilton's ice show for fear "they might depress" o t h e r paying customers. B o r g demanded an apology for the hotel manager's actions which came from owner-president Conrad Hilton, himself a member of the VFW. (Story on Page 2).

Dad's Druze funeral in Baakleen, 1967

the mass of flower bouquets was a wreath inscribed, "Farewell to our beloved chief." It was that farewell to the groceryman that brought tears.

This was to be a Masonic funeral. After a hush, a man holding a green shrub appeared in the aisle near where Mother and we were seated behind a shroud.

"With this evergreen ..." he began, then stopped.

He had forgotten his lines. From somewhere came a prompt. Beginning again he went as far as the prompt, where he paused again and received another prompt. I was laughing. Mother closed her eyes and I felt her talons pressing into my wrist. Dad would have laughed, I thought. No, not Dad. Grandfather. But he wasn't there. Dad had come every afternoon to ride him around town, Grandfather's only escape from his nurse and his gothic fortress on Woodlawn. Now frail and chair bound, he hadn't been told and he didn't ask.

Dad was buried. Uncle Jack became president. I produced a report outlining the modernization of the company.

"We're all for modernization," said Uncle Jack, "so long as it doesn't interfere with buying and selling groceries."

Everyone is for modernization but that was a euphemism for what was planned: total transformation. I was audacious and, with no ties to the past, loaded for bear. It was change ... or die.

And so it began. The store buildings and shopping centers were put in a separate corporation and the property director embarked on running it as a profit center. The local auditor was replaced by a national firm that began revamping and computerizing the information systems and accounting functions. Consultants were brought in for everything from the warehouse to the cardboard waste generated in the stores. Market research was conducted that showed the company's image had slipped and an institutional ad campaign was launched. A personnel director and controller who were more than bookkeepers were hired. The management was reorganized with job descriptions. By the Summer Dad's expansion was a footnote in the financial statement and people were laid off or given early retirement. The company was being transformed ...

... and it provoked a reaction. The clerical and maintenance people unionized. Uncle Jack was sought out by employees who voiced their complaints and insecurities. Several store managers called on Mother at her house to say that her son was going to ruin the company. She demanded that I come down to the company lawyer's office to answer this charge.

"What are you doing that those store managers should come to see me?!" she demanded. "And they want to unionize. This can't go on."

I listened, certain that what was being done had to be done if the company was to survive. But I was equally certain that what I had in strategy I lacked in sensitivity. Perhaps if I'd put myself in their place ... but I didn't. I was only in *my* place with Grandfather's oracle like an electric cattle prod behind me.

What should I answer? Mother shouldn't have received those managers, playing the memshaib and undercutting management but if I told her *that* she'd be indignant.... I was only doing what Dad should have done eons ago, I could have said, but she'd blow up and say no manager would have complained if he'd done it.... Of course, the managers, being management, weren't protected if they unionized but where would that have gotten me? ... I could have become indignant and declared if they didn't want the modernization I'd be pleased to go back to college, but I suspected she'd have been pleased to have me go....

"Mother, just hold off for two quarters and I guarantee you'll see the results in the profit and loss."

"The company could be ruined by then."

I hadn't thought of *that*. I turned to the company lawyer, inviting him to comment.

"You can wait one quarter for the financial results without jeopardizing the company," he advised her.

She nodded at me. One quarter, that's it! her expression declared.

In July, six months after Dad's death, Doris gave birth to our first child, a son. A month later I decided that taking Grandfather for his ride would be the occasion for him to meet his grandson. On the appointed day, Doris was at the Woodlawn house strolling *Lewie* outside. Inside, Grandfather was sitting in his chair, his arms hanging loosely off the sides, his hands shaking freely. He registered no recognition when he saw me. He began blinking rapidly as I took my son and placed him in his lap.

"*Hatha ibni*" I told him.

His eyes went from the child back to me and back again.

"*Ismoo* Lewie."

Did I wish him to understand that his grandson was Uncle Louie's namesake?

"I don't think he knows who you are," Doris said.

Grandfather peered up at me, earnest, questioning, as I took up Lewie.

"*Wynoo ibni?*" he asked clearly.

I stared at him.

"What did he say?" Doris asked.

"He's asking where is *his* son."

The nurse who had been observing from the entryway now came in with Grandfather's jacket and cap.

"That's the first time he's asked," she said, wrestling his arms into the sleeves. "He never talks, now that he stopped complaining. But he would never forget your father."

She pushed his motoring cap on his head and stood him up. "Robert Lee—your grandson—is going to take you for a nice ride now. You like that don't you? Of course you do."

She walked him to his Cadillac and settled him in. Then we were off, down Woodlawn to Court Street where we turned towards downtown. Off to the side was Flint Central High where I went for the tenth grade in zoot suit pants and white buck shoes and a duck's-ass haircut. Dad looked at my get-up and foresaw trouble. The following year I found myself in military school: up at 6:20am, feet on the floor at 6:23, out in ranks for inspection at 6:50.

Downtown Flint is Saginaw Street but we first had to pass by the majestic Capital Theater where Billy Geyer played organ during intermissions and where Mother went to watch Tyrone Power, whose picture she'd had in her bedroom in Ras el Metn.

Beneath the theater was Capital Recreation, an antiquated pool hall with unflushed urinals and occasional fights that was off-limits to me when I was fifteen. Uncle Joe being the only relative who played pool and poker was asked by Dad to keep an eye out for me and report back. Cousin Bob and I—the family distinguished us by calling me Lee Bob—never took a pool table near to where Uncle Joe drank and played cards. And he never saw us, a view I held until dear Uncle Joe passed on and willed me his pool cue.

If we'd turned north on Saginaw Street we would soon leave behind the banks and clothing stores for the bars and used car lots close by the Buick factory complex. We turned south and passed the courthouse and city jail on the right and, off to the left, the place where the Ojibway Indians brought in their medicinal bitters behind a team of horses. Dad and I stopped there once, maybe because their bitters had been sold in the stores. I watched him raise his hand and speak to them in their language. The three Ojibways made no response. When Dad got back into the car he said that, come to think about it, he was speaking Siouan, the language of their old enemies. And he went on to say that the Chippewas had once joined with their allies the Sauk and Fox and fought a great war against the Sioux and they got their ass kicked.

We were now passing our Michigan Theater store on the right.

"Hamady Bros., Zhidee!" I pointed and called out.

He looked but gave no sign of recognition. Was the company he created now lost to him? No. He knew. He didn't care. His love was elsewhere. I was thinking of his ride with Ted when he suddenly became animated, shaking one hand at Ted while the other was shaking in the direction of a horse out in the field. Ted pulled into a driveway and Grandfather gestured to get out. No sooner was he out than the horse started ambling over. A man came out of the house and stood by Ted to watch the horse nuzzle the old man. "That's Ebony Idol," he said. "That's Mike's old horse he had to give up 21 years ago."

We drove down South Saginaw and turned west. In the other direction was the A.C. Sparkplug plant, but here was the Fisher Body plant that was in my American History book because of the 1937 sitdown strike there that led to General Motors recognizing the Union. The U.A.W. had sent an emissary to Hamady

Soulmates

Bros. requesting free food for the strikers. Grandfather was probably amused when he asked why he should do that.

"You *know* me, Mike," the man said and Grandfather nodded. "My family was buying from you when you had the one store. We're your customers out there. We made you what you are. And now we need your help."

"How many truckloads do you want," Grandfather replied "and where do you want them?"

We soon turned north to drive up the West side of Flint, past Bishop Airport and the Ternstedt plant and finally onto Parkside Drive that curved around with the golf course to the Spanish style mansion we moved into when I was at college. I came home for the lavish party Dad and Mother held to inaugurate the house. They had recently joined the country club and the people coming would be different from the family and the assortment of ethnics we were familiar with. "They're coming up the drive," Dad, who didn't drink or smoke, said urgently. "Go ask William to mix you a Tom Collins. And you can smoke. In fact, light up. We want our guests to feel comfortable."

The house Ted and I grew up in north of the Chevrolet plant was not on our route. 1647 Neome Drive was where Mother imposed her restrictions on us. Stalag 1647 Ted later referred to it. I paid Mother back by not progressing on the violin. She'd seen the young prodigy, Yehudi Menuhin, in concert and envied Yehudi's mother. Minuet in G stayed my recital piece for two years and it would have been three if I hadn't been allowed to quit.

Close by the old home was our Third Avenue store where, beginning at age 13, I had to work weekends pecking potatoes and carrying out groceries for 25 cents an hour when the starting rate was 65 cents. The only real enjoyment I ever had there was the one time Dad came into the store when all the carryout boys were jostling for position to assist the voluptuous girl in a tight blue sweater with her one bag. He waved them off and motioned me over from where I was stacking lemons. I knew even then that I'd never work in the business. Now here I was, having to take Grandfather back because I had to get to the office.

The quarterly earnings reflecting the changes being made looked good enough to receive Mother's benediction. The modernization continued through the end of the year and well into 1968. Soon it was taking place against a backdrop of assassinations and race riots and angry crowds at the barricades.

Flying back from a business meeting in Chicago, the girl in the counter-culture hairdo and outfit sitting next to me took her attention from her book to ask if I'd watched the democratic convention.

"Did you see Mayor Daley's thugs tear into us with their clubs?" she asked. "We really showed America what pigs they are."

Not all of America. "I overheard a bunch of our employees watching it on their break," I told her, "and they were shouting for the police to 'kill 'em, kill those beards.' "

She took stock of my suit and tie and dismissed me with a turn back to her book. I smiled inside at her assumption that my comment and clothes stamped me as *one of them*. Then I saw my own assumption: that I *wasn't* one of them. "What's the matter, too good to be a businessman?" Dad asked in my mind. "And a grocery man, yet! Not ennobling enough? Too hard on the ego? ...

"Sit up straight! Straighten your hair! Don't pick your nose! All right, let's hear it."

"I'm a groceryman, Grandfather."

"Louder! Say it again! And this time look like you mean it."

"I'M A GROCERYMAN, GRANDFATHER!"

"That's more like it. Now you can be excused."

In December the moving finger wrote and Grandfather was dead. Strange, but I was going to miss him, that dapper old gentleman in his motoring cap who'd started with Kellogg's Corn Flakes and built it into a hundred million dollar sales company. The Flint Journal presented Ted and me with a bronze plaque inscribed with an article commemorating his life that had as its last words,

"There are many things by which Mr. Hamady will be remembered, ... but one facet of his career stands out beyond all others. It is his personal demonstration that opportunities are always open to Americans who have, not money or position, but fortitude and faith in the nation and its people."

When our daughter, Sarah, was born that February, Doris and I decided to buy the Woodlawn house and move to Flint. For the memories, I told Ted and we laughed. But he would never have moved there. Grandfather's presence permeated the living room; his oracle still echoed from the walls. No matter. It seemed as if I'd been expected, and had no choice but to come.

In Flint I didn't become a Rotarian and Doris didn't join the Junior League. I was on temporary duty. Our new friends included a gay couple with whom we shared a love for cooking. The rest were Jewish. We fit, and I saw Mother in my friend Ben's mother, who had on her bathroom door a poster of cancer's seven

The Flint Journal

Year—No. 270   2 Sections—26 Pages   Flint, Mich.   Zip Code 48502⁻¹   Monday, December 30, 1968   CE 4-7611 (Want Ads CE 4-7651)   Price: 7c

Very Rosy
More Rain Likely:
Cooler by Tuesday
Details, Page 15

Area Residents Without Heat
Details, Page 15

MICHAEL HAMADY, 84, DIES

Michael H. Hamady—Flint's "Mr. Grocer"

Michael H. Hamady, Flint's most widely known grocer, died in his sleep Sunday at his home. He was 84.

Private services for relatives and close friends will be at 1 p.m. Tuesday in the Algoe Funeral Home. Dr. David E. Molyneaux, pastor of First Presbyterian Church, will officiate. Burial will be in Sunset Hills.

As founder and co-chairman of the board of directors of the Hamady Bros. Inc., Mr. Hamady rightly claimed the title of Flint's leading grocer even though he had been inactive for several years.

He is credited as being a pioneer in the self-serve food market and linked food shopping with Flint's own product, the automobile. His stores early were tabbed "automobile" shoppers' food markets.

He was a leader in the development of what now are called "supermarkets," and was recognized by the food industry as such.

Since his first market at E. Dayton Street and Industrial Avenue opened in 1911, Mr. Hamady steered Hamady Bros. to a dominant area food chain of 27 stores.

These include stores in Fenton, Holly, Lapeer, Davison, Grand Blanc, Swartz Creek, Mt. Morris and Lansing. Two more stores are to be opened in Lansing in 1969.

Through his firm he long supported 4-H activity in Genesee County, by purchasing prize stock and publicizing the efforts of blue-ribbon winners in local circles.

His company has won many trade honors and Mr. Hamady was accorded a place in the "Hall of Fame" of the Detroit Food Brokers Association.

He also carried the Detroit Lebanese Business Clubs Association's 1961 award for

civic, humanitarian and civic betterment achievements.

Mr. Hamady always felt greatly indebted to and appreciative of his "new land" and was generous in demonstrating his love for this country.

He and his firm each gave $25,000 sponsorships to the Flint College and Cultural Development.

His $175,000 Hamady House estate on Branch Road, which was given to the Mott Foundation in 1943 has become a local institution. It serves the Mott Programs through which young girls are prepared for future roles as homemakers and mothers.

He gave 15 acres to the Westwood Heights School District in 1961 and added five acres to a 30-acre site his firm gave the district some years before that. The district's elementary, high and junior high schools are named for him.

In 1964, Mr. Hamady gave $150,000 to Hurley Hospital for a new medical library. It is named for him. He called the gift "a mark of my own appreciation of the fine city in which we live."

Mr. Hamady founded the

grocery chain with a distant relative, Kamol C. Hamady. He was president of the company until 1964, when his son, the late Robert M. Hamady, was elected to the post. Robert died in 1966.

As board chairman and major stockholder of the company, however, he continued to help shape the growth of the firm. Last year, a grandson, Theodore M. Hamady, was named co-chairman of the board.

Mr. Hamady was born in Baskinté, Lebanon, and came to this country in 1908. He came to Flint from Caro in 1909.

He leaves his daughter-in-law, Mrs. Robert M. Hamady, Flint; a second grandson, Robert L. Hamady, Fenton; three great-grandsons, and several nieces and nephews. A second son died in 1928.

Related articles and photos on page 15.

Israel Vows More Attacks

Associated Press

Israel appeared headed by mounting condemnation from all sides of its border for another tough Israeli-Arab clash. The Beirut government "strongly condemns" the raid...

night and appeared headed for reported that President John Lebanon, Dwight Eisenhower, called mandos destroyed 13 Lebanese...

The U.S. Ambassador to Lebanon said Yaïl to discuss how the United States could help Lebanon...

3 Helicopters Shot Down By Viet Cong

danger signals. No one was a zealot so there were no *sides* when we discussed the Middle East.

In May I was called down to the company attorney's office.

"Who the hell is running the company?" he demanded. "Jack is directing daily operations and you're making all those changes. I'm receiving complaints and hearing grumbling. It's no longer workable. There can only be one boss."

This was bad news. I didn't want a title that would bind me closer to the company's fortunes. But those fortunes depended on the modernization taking place. And *that* couldn't be entrusted to anyone else. If there had to be a change,

"It's got to be me."

X

Who should be president? That would be decided by the five persons who voted Grandfather's controlling interest and so, ruled the company: Mother, her accountant, the company attorney, Ted and me.

When the meeting was convened, Mother suggested that someone should be brought in from the outside to be president.

RULE. IT IS BETTER FOR BROTHERS TO BOW TO A TURK THAN FOR ONE TO BOW TO THE OTHER.

Uncle Jack was present and suggested that an industrial psychologist be selected by our director of personnel to evaluate Ted, me and himself for the presidency. I replied that we all knew each other and shouldn't leave that decision to a stranger.

The vote was four to one for the psychologist.

Soon, a consultant from a recognized New York firm arrived to conduct interviews with us and seek opinions from others in top management. He spent a half-hour with me, asking generic questions without probing for answers. When his report was completed, we were reconvened at the attorney's office. The recommendations:

In Jack Hamady the company is fortunate to have the right and best man as C.E.O.;

Ted Hamady has a contribution to make and should grow in the business;

Bob Hamady is a college boy who is out of place in business. As president he would be a disaster for the company.

"The blood would run in the streets if he were president," someone had said. He should leave and return to college.

No one spoke. My God! What a condemnation! So explicit and insistent. I was stunned. And Mother! She had to wonder: to whom had she entrusted the remaking of Hamady Bros?!

Said the company attorney, "I think we had all better go home and let this sink in."

Driving home I was philosophical, and not unhappy. The university was where I wanted to be, after all. And since *they* were rejecting *me*, I could continue my studies without feeling like a draft dodger ...

... Still, that a stranger could waltz in, issue his condemnation, and have it accepted as gospel! Was I really the wolf? Or were they a bunch of sheep?

Doris laughed when she learned, imagining me sitting there unmasked, "like a Norway rat at a sanitation meeting," she said. We began making plans for our return to Ann Arbor.

The following morning I arrived late to my office. The property director was waiting inside. He was wide-eyed with impending news.

"The personnel secretary is a friend and she called me on the sly," he began, dramatically. "'I think you ought to know' is how she put it. That psychologist who evaluated you all? He was no stranger."

He was nodding. And then we both were nodding. They knew each other. Our personnel director and the psychologist he selected knew each other. But that was the sort of thing that only went on in larger corporations, wasn't it?

"Do you think it had Uncle Jack's blessing?" he asked.

"If it *is* a setup." I replied in my legal voice.

"If it is a setup?" he repeated.

"Uncle Jack?" I began and paused "... Uncle Jack and Dad and Dad's brother and their mothers all slept in the same big bed in the old country. Did you know that? ..."

He was waiting.

"... No, Uncle Jack has no involvement. And that's a fact."

"That's a fact," he repeated. "What about *our* director of personnel? *He* wasn't in the bed."

I was shaking my head. Let sleeping dogs lie, I thought. For now.

Well, well. I called the company attorney with the news. "That evaluation is tainted," he said. "There will be another one, and this time, the auditors will select."

We may not be moving, I told Doris.

One month passed and then a Dr. Adams arrived to conduct a week of tests and interviews. Arthur Andersen, the auditors, guaranteed his objectivity. Some weeks later we met for his recommendations. What we now heard was,

"Make Mr. Robert Lee Hamady the only executive vice president as soon as possible.... Schedule him for the Harvard Business School three month resident course for senior executives.... Shortly after completion Mr. Robert Lee Hamady would be made president."

Uncle Jack reached a hand over and we shook hands. Mother was nodding, seemingly more surprised by this evaluation than the damning one.

"Well," said the company attorney looking around, "now we can all go home."

But less than a month later and before any preparations had been made for Harvard, the company attorney called, saying that Mother and her accountant felt I should be given the title now.

"Mother?"

"Your brother and I vote against it," he said. "How do you vote?"

"Congratulate me," I told him. "I'm the new C.E.O."

The transition was made with little fanfare. I moved into the big office and put my things in the desk drawers and my papers in the credenza behind. I brought in my espresso pot and hung Doris' abstract expressionist painting. I lit my pipe and leaned back in the leather swivel chair. I was in *his* chair. And I had only to open the right bottom desk drawer to see the loaves of Syrian bread that I could roll into cylinders and eat as he did.

Sitting there, presiding over supermarkets and shopping centers and a thousand employees, I could feel the power he so loved seeping up through the chair. And I had it all right, not from the title but from Dr. Adam's report. When he wrote of me, "As a business strategist he can become hard to beat," that was seen to validate all of the changes made to the business. And as proof of the power of "expert" testimonial, even *Mother* now deferred to me. "I wanted you to get the credit for what you've done for the company," she said to me. "That's why John and I made you chief executive now instead of after Harvard."

But I wouldn't be CEO for long. I'd seen Grandfather's and Dad's estates and I knew the other major stockholdings were similar. After paying off debt and estate tax, all they'd have after a half-century of work was a company oversaturated in its market area that was dependent on one corporation, even if that corporation was the world's largest. Perhaps if I needed the power, or the business had a sustainable competitive edge that would justify expansion … but we didn't.

—Journal Photo

EXECUTIVE LINEUP — New officers were elected this week for Hamady Bros., Inc. and Hamady Bros. Food Markets., Inc. They are (from left) Jack M. Hamady, chairman of the boards of both companies; Robert Lee Hamady, president and chief executive officer of both companies; Theodore M. Hamady, executive vice president of Hamady Bros. Food Markets, Inc.; and Donald J. Skarritt, executive vice president of Hamady Bros., Inc. The firm has 26 outlets in the Flint area.

New Officers Are Elected For Two Hamady Companies

Robert Lee Hamady was elected president and chief executive officer of Hamady Bros., Inc., and Hamady Bros. Food Markets, Inc. at a meeting of the board of directors this week.

Hamady Bros., Inc., the parent corporation, is primarily involved in administering the company's real estate properties, and the food markets subsidiary operates the 26 Hamady supermarkets.

Theodore M. Hamady was elected executive vice president of Hamady Bros. Food Markets, Inc. and Donald J. Skarritt was named executive vice president of Hamady Bros., Inc.

Jack A. Hamady, whose term as president and chief executive officer of both companies expired at the meeting, was named chairman of the board, which serves both companies.

Both Theodore M. and Robert Lee Hamady are sons of the late Robert M. Hamady, for years president of the company, and grandsons of the cofounder, the late Michael M. Hamady.

Robert Lee is a 1958 graduate of Northwestern University and has a degree from the University of Michigan Law School. He previously had been executive vice president and director of corporate planning, advertising and research.

Theodore joined the firm in 1960 after graduation from the University of Michigan. He had been in charge of grocery buying and merchandising.

Skarritt joined the firm in 1967 as director of property. He was elected a corporate vice president in 1968 and a director in 1969. He is a graduate of the University of Michigan.

The business was being transformed ... to sell it. My objective had been reluctantly accepted within the inner circle but it was emotionally charged. Like Dad, Uncle Jack was hoping to die in the business. Ted would be cut loose to face the unknown. And for Mother, selling Hamady Bros. was selling the church. Dad's spirit resided within these walls. Unless the sale price was extraordinary, they would never accept it.

Less than a week after moving into Dad's office I pushed my finger into the moving flywheel of my Porsche, and when I examined it the fingertip was gone. Surgery was required. Why should I have done such a thing? Dr. Kimbrough provided the explanation. "That was penance for daring to take your father's place. No question. And your atonement may be ongoing ... so be careful."

My finger was still in a wrap when the personnel director asked to see me. The controller, he said, was stepping out with his secretary, which was cause for dismissal. The revelation had come via one of his informants. When I put the charge to the controller he denied it. The personnel director reentered and asked whom I believed.

"I believe you," I told him, "But I don't think you fit in here. I think you're better suited to a large corporation."

He slumped back in his chair, staring hard at me.

"Oh, I see," he said with a smirk. "All right. Can we put it that I'm resigning?"

"No, because you're not."

The notice was posted and was followed by cheering in the hall. I made no connection. The warehouse manager threw open my door.

"That's the best fucking thing you've ever done. Did you hear that cheering? That son-of-a-bitch was ordering everyone around and threatening them with his connection to Jack."

Then, seeing my unaware expression, "He had his own fiefdom going!"

I had no idea. Too involved with abstractions, I decided. A college boy president.

The 1970s began with a General Motors strike and sales stagnated throughout Eastern Michigan. The Vietnam War dragged on and inflation steepened, as customers could see by the two and three price increases stamped on the canned goods. A store manager reported overhearing one customer with a full food cart saying that somebody ought to kill those Hamadys. President Nixon ordered a price freeze but labor cost increases had to be absorbed. Business responded with across the board discounting and gross margins shrank. The stock markets were gyrating. Rumors flew of grocery chains going under or ceasing operations in Flint and Detroit.

Hamady Bros. had been remade. A new merchandising management had been brought in from outside and a profit-sharing plan established. A consultant was directing team planning and goal setting. After seeing the company's financial history he informed me that Grandfather had the overview and was the general while Dad was the good, loyal lieutenant. That soured me. He was belittling the prominent man in town who had visited my elementary school to address us about traffic safety, making me so proud ... and belittling the father who could beat up the fathers of all the boys I didn't beat. Maybe I'd made him up, refigured him from his best parts, discarding the others, and created the father I needed to sustain me until I grew up. But *he* had sustained me. And I didn't want to hear anyone putting him down.

I now embarked on selling the family business. In New York two investment bankers tried and failed to sell the property. Sale of the grocery company was agreed upon with a food wholesaler in Chicago but its stock price dropped precipitously, scotching the deal. A Detroit food chain was interested on condition the rents and lease terms were altered: no deal. A merger with Borman Foods out of Detroit that owned our largest tenant appeared likely but their stock value was dropping and eventually fell eighty percent. Two years passed and I was shaking my head. I feel like a hapless whore, I told Doris.

Then in early 1973 our new attorney in Detroit said he had two investors from Pittsburgh who wanted to inspect the property. This they did, posing as insurance investigators. We then met at the attorney's office at 5:00pm. The prospective purchasers had charts of our properties laid out with columns for leaks, cracks, aging, etc. The columns that intrigued me were marked:

Termite soldiers

Dead reproductives

Nymphs

Eggs

Tunnels

Each nymph and tunnel had to be discussed and a reduction to the asking price negotiated. At 3:00am a recess was called.

"These guys are the Pittsburgh Stealers," said our property director. "If they find a termite queen we're going to end up owing *them* money."

"Stick with these guys," the attorney said. "They're deal makers."

We did, and at 6:00am the property was sold.

I went home to sleep and didn't arrive at the office until mid-afternoon. No announcement of the sale had been made but the word was out.

"Are you taking calls?" my secretary asked.

I took the phone.

"I own some shares of Hamadys," a voice said. "It was quoted at eight dollars a share last I looked and I just heard you sold the property for twenty-one dollars a share. Is that right? And we still own the grocery business? Can you explain it to me?"

I was reflecting as he spoke. No one pulls a rabbit from a hat unless the rabbit is in the hat. Grandfather didn't see that what he'd built was a property company. Dad, too. They were grocerymen. I had fantasized that when this moment came—because Grandfather's prophecy now was self-made man hot air—my reaction would be exhilaration, or I'd simply take up my pipe and luxuriate. Instead, I was RELIEVED. Like the boy who didn't know his father drank until he saw him sober, only now with the burden lifted did I *feel* what was at stake.

There remained the grocery company. It hummed efficiently, unaware what was being plotted, because it had to be disposed of or distributed within a year to avoid a double tax. A fifty thousand dollar finder's fee was discretely offered to whoever finds the buyer.

That summer Doris and I moved to Washington, D.C. where several cousins had preceded us but I was remaining C.E.O. until the final liquidation.

In October, Uncle Jack was notified of an interested investor, but one who might be connected to the mafia. The company lawyer was asked to investigate. When he advised there was no connection I invited the man to see the company. He did and was impressed. An agreement was quickly drawn up.

Now with sale imminent, Mother wavered.

"How can you sell the business now that you have it the way you want it?" she exclaimed and held out a letter. "Look what John has to say about it."

The letter was from her accountant.

"Just a memo to cheer you up a bit. I realize that the sale of the real estate is a trying experience for you; especially when the sale of the food markets is also just around the corner. . . . The sale of the real estate is a good thing for you financially and more so in that your son Bob really engineered the deal. . . . Bob is not deserting the grocery stores. Operations under Ray and his staff are as good if not better than any comparable operation in the country. . . ."

"But Mother, I'm not interested in staying in the business."

"What are you going to be without it?" she asked. "Once its gone, . . ."

She trailed off and there was grief in her eyes that was giving way to tears. I put my arms around her and for me, too, there were tears. Love is care, I heard Dad saying: Now you know . . . Not so, I told myself. It's only a business. Bricks and mortar. But the tears knew the truth and ran freely down my cheeks.

On the day of the signing, first thing, I reminded myself that selling was in the best interests of the stockholders. At the steps up to the lawyer's office I hesitated just long enough to turn off my receptors lest I hear cries of protest from the grave. Then I went in and signed away the grocery business.

Afterwards, walking out with the property director, he asked how it felt to give away the mosque. I'm cold blooded, I told him. But that was a half-truth. The business hadn't vanished. It would live on as Hamady Bros. How important that now seemed.

Still, there had been something strange at the signing: a tough-looking round faced bald man in padded shoulders and pointed toe shoes. He looked like he'd wandered off the set of *On the Waterfront*.

"A bodyguard, do you think?" I asked.

"Bodyguards don't sign the documents," he replied.

That's right, he did! Did he represent mob money and the purchaser was a front man? ... I smiled, imagining the first ad.

"HAMADY BROS. PASSES ON ITS SKIMMING SAVINGS TO YOU."

The levity didn't last. Who were those guys?

I was soon driving Mother's car back to Mother. Once in her driveway I angled the car to the side out of sight and sat. It was Dad. His spirit was afoot. If he could return.... I could hear him. "DAMN YOU for selling the business. And damn me for ever wanting you in it." And then if he caught sight of the new owners?! He'd charge me, as he'd done in the past....

"Not this time, Dad," I said out loud, as if warning him that now he could expect a brawl.

Because I didn't regret the sale. Was that all he cared about: the business? The hell with it! Why should a business endure as the shrine and his brother, who was sacrificed for it, be buried somewhere and forgotten? Uncle Louie had my son as

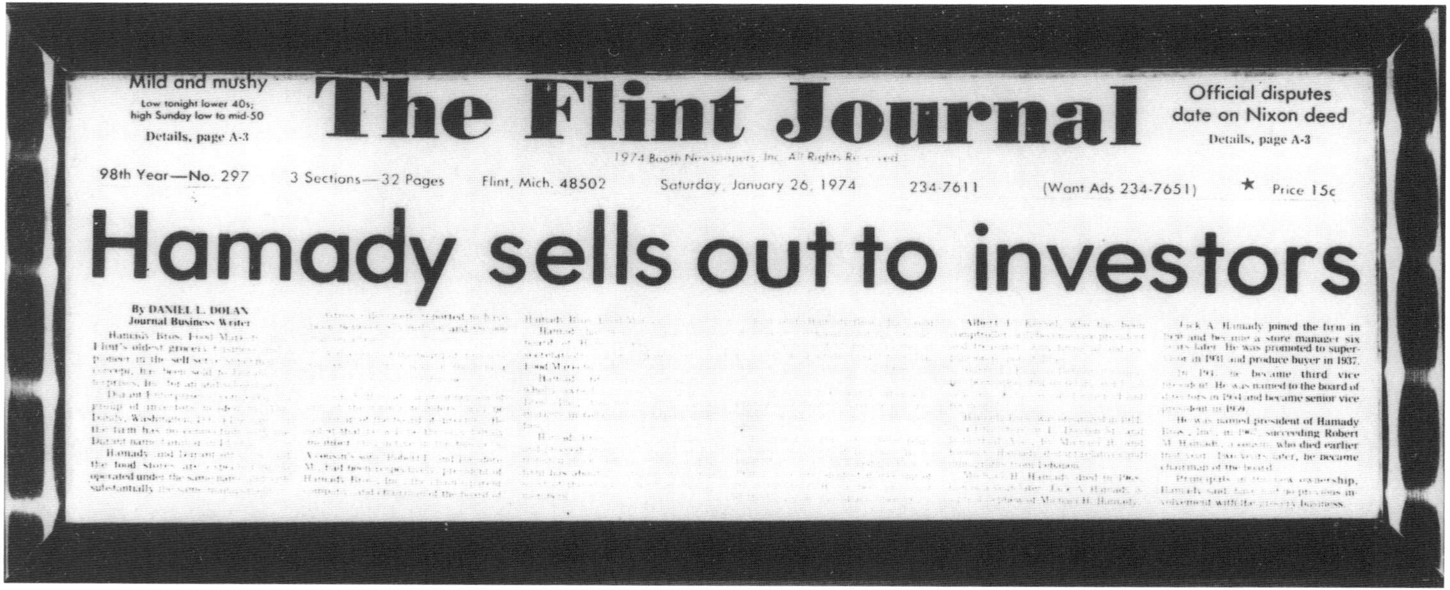

Mild and mushy
Low tonight lower 40s;
high Sunday low to mid-50

Details, page A-3

98th Year—No. 297   3 Sections—32 Pages   Flint, Mich. 48502   Saturday, January 26, 1974   234.7611

1974 Booth Newspapers, Inc. All Rights Reserved

(Want Ads 234-7651)   ★   Price 15c

Official disputes
date on Nixon deed

Details, page A-3

The Flint Journal

Hamady sells out to investors

By DANIEL L. DOLAN
Journal Business Writer

his namesake, his legacy. Dad would just have to make do now with Ted and me. If that left him unsatisfied ... then to hell with him, too.

As my ire subsided I was again feeling sorry for Dad. I supposed I always would. But now I had to bridge the breach between us in my mind. I had to give his spirit repose in some way. But how? ...

Grandfather could do it. Dad would listen to him. Yes, and he had something that trumps the business. So, ...

If Grandfather said to him,

"When I came here in 1908, poor and couldn't speak English, the grocery business opened its arms to me, just as it did to every immigrant—Arabs and Jews, Chinese and Italians— because with one month's rent and two cartons of Kelloggs Corn Flakes I could be a grocery man. And if I didn't speak the language I could introduce self serve....

"But when I came back here with you and Louie it wasn't the grocery business I kissed. Remember? Hamady Bros.—any grocery business—is merely the most faithful representative of this country. Before getting into that taxi in New York, I got down and kissed the ground. *This* ground. *That's* our business, Robert. That's what you and I helped to make, and what in turn made us....

"What am I talking about, son?"

Dad will smile.

"What else? America. And it's still here."

XI

It had been a year and a half now since the business was sold. Ted had moved to D.C. Uncle Frank divorced Aunt Thelma and went down to Florida. Most of my relatives had left Flint for the East and West Coasts and even for Lebanon. Those who remained were unconnected except for the occasional encounter and ceremony. The family, like the family business, was gone.

Ted was pursuing a Master's Degree in business. He'll be the one who takes after Dad. I was going the other way. I'd started a consulting business to help public school systems develop strategic planning and we quickly had clients nationally. But that entailed a life on the road, and in a motel room in Frankfort, Kentucky, I resolved to find a pursuit I enjoyed. But what? After the drama at Hamady Bros., university life seemed monastic and bloodless. I'd changed. Perhaps at some gathering I might hear myself declaring,

"Them that can, do. And them that can't, teach."

Lord, save me from becoming *that*!

Five months ago, I'd turned thirty-nine. My jog had evolved into the knee-pumping motion of the middle-aged man. A colon probe was added to my physical examination and to prepare I had to purchase a *Fleet's enema*. I told the pharmacist it was the *Fleets* I was unfamiliar with. He opened the box and took out a device a few inches long. Compared to Mother's screaming eagle rubber water bottle which when filled resembled a rugby ball, this thing looked like what a pet store would have on hand to relieve a constipated pug. No, the pharmacist said, it didn't inflate. And there were no other parts, no hoses or reservoirs. And, yes, it would move me. So! The dose I'd been given when I was eight was what a wildlife biologist would use to clean out a hibernating bear.

I was sitting now with Mother on the porch of Grandfather's 1886 cottage on Mackinac Island, enjoying the view across the West bluff to the old lighthouse. If I confronted her with the enemas she'd just laugh and say, "Oh, Bobby, where do you come up with these notions?" But look who had the notions. Almost her first words when we arrived were, "You know, Bobby, there are so many bats on Mackinac that they're hanging from the ceiling." And if I'd told her that one bat will hang from the ceiling she'd have said she wasn't talking about just one bat. With reasoning like that she was forever protected from feeling regret.

"I can't believe you boys sold the business," she said now without looking up from her magazine, as if she'd just received the news.

That was a black hole and I wasn't getting near it. Doris would be down soon with our one year old, Leslie, and we could go have a cocktail at the Iroquois.

"Your poor father, if he were alive!"

What was she reading, anyway?!

"Your grandfather, he said it would happen. *He* knew."

"You came out all right," I heard myself tell her. "What do you have to complain about?"

"Money isn't everything. If you and your brother had what it takes—"

"You don't know what you're talking about."

"I know that if your father was alive—"

"He was over his head. The business was in terrible shape."

Her eyes opened wide with anger. "The business in terrible shape? Not until he got sick and you and your brother took over."

"You don't know what you're talking about."

"I don't, huh? Your father came up through the ranks working 12 hours a day, seven days a week. He made that business. You and your brother come along and sell it. And why? To inherit your money."

I was on my feet. "You don't know what in the hell you're talking about! Now you listen. Dad got out at the right time. He let that business run on too long as a one-man show...."

"Listen!" I shouted because she wanted to interrupt. "When I came into that business there were so many problems I wanted to fly out in all directions. You see that company that we just sold? I made it. Who do you think would have been blamed if it had failed? I *made* that company. I willed it to succeed. So don't give me that crap that I inherited the money. God damn it, I earned it!"

Mother was silent. She brought her hand slowly to her cheek and regarded me in astonishment.

"My God, Bobby," she began, breathless. "You're just like your grandfather. You're just like him.... You're INSUFFERABLE."

She was right, and I was laughing.

"Did you hear *that*, Dr. Kimbrough? I know who I am."

God be praised.

I was cured.

EPILOGUE

Hamady Bros. was liquidated in 1991 after being bilked and bankrupted by the investor purchaser who received a 23-year prison sentence. A Hamady store sign survives in Flint's Sloan Museum in an exhibit called *Flint and the American Dream.*

Thanks, Marianne Garman, for your loving support

Washington, D.C.